On the Buses:
The Filming Locations

By Craig Walker

ON THE BUSES:
THE FILMING LOCATIONS
by
Craig Walker

Copyright © 2016

ISBN: 978-0-9934532-1-2

This book is published by Caledonian Books Limited in conjunction with **WRITERSWORLD**, and is produced entirely in the UK. It is available to order from most bookshops in the United Kingdom, and is also globally available via UK based Internet book retailers.

WRITERSWORLD
2 Bear Close Flats, Bear Close, Woodstock
Oxfordshire, OX20 1JX, England
☎ 01993 812500
☎ +44 1993 812500

www.writersworld.co.uk

The text pages of this book are produced via an independent certification process that ensures the trees from which the paper is produced come from well managed sources that exclude the risk of using illegally logged timber while leaving options to use post-consumer recycled paper as well.

Photographs

Contents

Acknowledgements

There are many people to thank for their input into this project, such as those who have helped with information with regards to filming locations. Robert Hickey – a lifelong resident of Borehamwood – identified a number of locations in the town and that help has been important and much appreciated. A few years ago I ran a forum dedicated to *On the Buses* and many forum members (too many to mention by name) helped to find a few locations dotted around London and in North Wales and that was a great help. I also thank those kind enough to email me personally identifying previously unknown filming locations. A massive thank you must go to Richard Coghill who, along with myself, spent many hours scouring the episodes and films, studying London and beyond on software such as Google Street View and then visiting identified possible locations for confirmation. It really was invaluable help for such a large-scale project.

Out on my travels, help came from unexpected sources such as an employee at the Palace Fun Centre in Rhyl called Jane – an *On the Buses* fan as well. Her information cleared up confusion as to the location of the scenes filmed on the seafront in *Holiday on the Buses* and so a big thank you to her as well as the time and advice offered by the Rhyl Tourist Information Centre. Also I'd like to thank staff at Pontin's Prestatyn Sands Holiday Park for their help, patience and assistance in giving me access to out of bounds areas to allow me to garner photographs. Likewise, thanks to those permitting me to take photographs at the Chiswick Business Park (former site of London Transport's Chiswick Skid Pan facility) as well as park wardens for their help and hospitality on Peckham Common – it really was appreciated.

I must also thank residents for their understanding and for allowing me to photograph properties across London, Borehamwood and in North Wales. Without their co-operation in allowing me freedom to photograph these locations this book would not have been possible.

Also I must thank StudioCanal Plus for allowing me access and permission to use their vast archive of images whose photographs you can see scattered throughout the book and also similar thanks to Rex Features for use of photographs in the production of this book.

Introduction

The book you are about to read catalogues many filming locations used for the hugely successful sitcom *On the Buses*, which ran from 1969 until 1973. Fans of the television series and spin-off films not only love to watch the classic comedy – they also love to hunt down filming locations for fun and visit them to retrace the steps made by the many great actors and actresses when filming their much-loved television series or films.

I am no different and in my case my love of this classic sitcom has inspired me to write this book which will take you on a tour of the many filming locations used in all seven series of the television series and the three spin-off films, with photographs displaying the locations as they look today.

On the Buses first hit our television screens in 1969 with the series being filmed by London Weekend Television (also known as LWT) at their Wembley Studios. The first six series were filmed here and external filming locations were dotted around North London, normally in close proximity to the studios in suburbs including Wembley, Hendon, Enfield and Wood Green. In late 1972, LWT relocated to their new custom-built studios at the South Bank Television Centre Studios on the south bank of the River Thames. It was here that series seven was to be filmed and filming locations were to be found in areas such as Battersea, Lambeth, Peckham and Morden amongst others.

Of course, *On the Buses* also spawned three spin-off films which were to be filmed at the EMI-MGM Elstree Studios in the Hertfordshire town of Borehamwood, which was located a few miles to the north of London. The first film, simply called *On the Buses*, released in 1971, was shot chiefly in the nearby streets of the town and also in the village of Shenley a few miles to the north-east of the studios. A year later the second spin-off film, *Mutiny on the Buses* was filmed in similar locations in the town but also expanded further afield to film at a popular tourist attraction of the time – Windsor Safari Park. In 1973 came the third and final spin-off film, *Holiday on the Buses*, which was shot once more around Borehamwood but chiefly on location at the Welsh seaside resort of Prestatyn in North Wales and in surrounding towns and villages. This was to be the furthest afield that the cast and crew ventured to film *On the Buses* on either the small or big screen in the four years of its lifespan.

Since *On the Buses* was made well over 40 years ago, unearthing filming locations can prove very challenging. Much can and has changed in all of that time, with redevelopment of locations commonplace, and so to help track some and pinpoint them with a degree of certainty it always pays to scrutinise the smallest details, however irrelevant they may seem. Houses can change appearance or be demolished but often trees remain as do other features such as lamp posts, telegraph poles, electricity pylons and other permanent structures. As you will see in this book many of the filming locations need the presence of trees and such-like to help with identification when the rest of the area has changed so much in appearance.

Hopefully, this book will answer a few questions in revealing where some of the most iconic scenes were filmed. With photos giving you a look at how these locations look today it will also explain in detail how to find and visit these points of interest and exactly in which episode or film they appeared and at what moment. If you wish to visit *On the Buses* filming locations then this book will be the perfect guide for you. I hope you enjoy it as much as it has been for me in compiling it.

Chapter One – The Wembley Years

Location 1: The Former LWT Studios

Series Two until the end of Series Six

128 Wembley Park Drive, Wembley, London, HA9 8HP.

Since the late 1920s, studios have stood on this site in Wembley in one form or another. It all began with humble beginnings with a one stage studio called the Wembley National Studios. After a fire in 1929, the studios came under new ownership and film production continued under varying guises such as British Talking Pictures, Fox-British Pictures and various independent film production companies up until the mid-1950s.

In 1955, the studios underwent large-scale refurbishments under the new ownership of Associated-Rediffusion who set about converting the facility into a television production studio after decades of film production. Despite financial problems, Stage 5 was built in 1960 and the company, part of ITV, were to produce classic TV series such as *The Dickie Henderson Show*, *Ready Steady Go*, *Educating Archie*, *Take Your Pick*, *No Hiding Place* and *Double Your Money* through until the late 1960s.

In May 1968, London Weekend Television (also known as LWT) were to take over ITV's London weekend television franchise, leasing the Wembley studios from Rediffusion (Associated having been dropped from their title in 1964). On Stage 5 on Friday the 20th June 1969 at 8pm, the studios recorded the first episode of *On the Buses* in front of a live audience and the studios would remain home to the hit sitcom for six series. Other hit LWT series to be produced at Wembley included *Hark at Barker*, *Doctor on the Go*, *Please Sir*, *Upstairs Downstairs*, *Frost on Sunday* and *The Fenn Street Gang*. During their stay, LWT refurbished the studios further before vacating the premises by the end of 1972.

For a number of years the studios remained inactive until 1978 when the Lee brothers bought the facility and renamed them the Lee International Film Studios. They reconverted the studios into a film production facility and films to come out of them included

Quadrophenia, *The Elephant Man*, *Time Bandits* and *Brazil*. The brothers had also acquired Shepperton Studios and by the summer of 1986 they had vacated the Wembley site.

A further three years of inactivity followed before Limehouse Television bought the site, announcing ambitious plans for the studios which included creating a vast media site to be built following demolition of a part of the old film studios. However, this did not materialise, as a retail park was instead built on that part of the site whilst the studios were refurbished as television production was once more on the agenda. The studios would produce hit series for both the BBC and ITV including *Food and Drink*, *You Bet*, *Whose Line Is It Anyway?* and *Have I Got News for You?* However, late in 1992, the parent company of Limehouse Television went bust and their hold on the studios was lost.

The studios fell into disrepair and when Fountain Television took over the site in 1993 a lot of hard work was required to make the studios operational again. The facility became Fountain Studios and in 1994 television productions began for both BBC and ITV. The studios boast productions such as *Hearts of Gold*, *Test the Nation*, *Pop Idol*, *The Cube*, *Over the Rainbow* and *The X-Factor* among others. Fountain Studios had been active at Wembley for over 20 years, making them the longest tenant at the studios in its long history but very sad news broke in January 2016 that a property developer had bought the site for £16 million with the studios earmarked to be demolished after almost a century in service.

How to get there: The most direct route to this location is via tube from either King's Cross/St Pancras Station on the Metropolitan Line or from Waterloo on the Jubilee Line, both heading northbound to Wembley Park. Exit Wembley Park Tube Station, cross the road and turn right to walk down Wembley Park Drive for 200 metres and you will find Fountain Studios on your left.

By bus the most direct route is from Stop H at London Euston Station aboard the No. 18 bus to Sudbury. Change at Wembley Central Station and board either the No. 223 (to Harrow) or No. 182 bus (Brent Cross) from Stop CM and disembark at Stop G (Wembley Arena) on Wembley Park Drive and walk 150 metres north. Fountain Studios will be on your right at the junction of Fulton Road.

Now

Fountain Studios (former home of LWT).

The rear access to Fountain Studios where the Lodekka buses used to enter through to gain access into the studios when leased by LWT.

Location 2: Start of the Opening Credits in Series One

Series One, Episode One: *The Early Shift*

Wembley Park Drive, Wembley, London, HA9 8HD.

As the opening credits (which are used throughout the first series) begin to roll on the first episode, for the first ten seconds we see Stan's bus driving along a curved road lined by houses with a distinctive house on the junction of a road in the background. That house was to be the focal point for the search and although, today, it is masked somewhat by trees in the garden in front of it, I used the house to trace this location. It is less than half a mile away from the Wembley Studios where *On the Buses* was being filmed at this time and was ideal and very convenient. Today the location hasn't changed too much aside from a new house being built on the left-hand side of the road and trees now more of a feature. Stan's bus would have been filmed passing Nos. 11, 13 and 15 Wembley Park Drive before cutting to another shot as it passed No. 17 Wembley Park Drive.

How to get there: The most direct route to this location is via tube from either King's Cross/St Pancras Station on the Metropolitan Line or from Waterloo on the Jubilee Line, both heading northbound to Wembley Park. Exit Wembley Park Tube Station, turn right and walk down Wembley Park Drive for 600 metres and you will find the location on the curve of Wembley Park Drive by the house numbered 17.

By bus the most direct route is from Stop H at Euston Station aboard the No. 18 to Sudbury. Change at Wembley Central Station and board the No. 297 from Stop CN and disembark at Stop M (Balmoral Court) at 35 Wembley Park Drive and from here it is a short walk of 50 metres to the location, heading back in the direction the bus has brought you.

Then

Now

Wembley Park Drive - scene of the opening credits.

Location 3: End of the Opening Credits in Series One

Series One, Episode One: *The Early Shift*

Alexandra Park Road, Wood Green, London, N10 2DG.

The opening credits of Series One continue to roll and (10 to 25 seconds into the credits) a bus is seen travelling down a road lined by houses on both sides of the road towards Mum who stands at a bus stop. This scene was filmed on Alexandra Park Road with Mum standing east of the junction to Grasmere Road and the clues to this location were the three-storied houses on the left side of the road, the turret-like structure on a house to the right of the bus stop and the steep inclining road with a sharp turn to the left at the top. All are present at this location and it has remained much the same to the present day.

How to get there: The most direct route to this location is via tube from King's Cross/St Pancras Station on the Northern Line heading northbound to Golders Green. Exit Golders Green Station, turn right and from Stop GU board the No. 102 (to Edmonton Green Bus Station). Disembark at Stop CR (St. Andrew's Church) and turn right and walk 100 metres along Alexandra Park Road until having just crossed Grasmere Road where the camera would have filmed this scene looking back in the direction you have just travelled.

By bus the most direct route is from Stop C outside London Euston Station aboard the No. 390 (to Archway). Disembark at Stop AP (Archway) and turn right to walk five metres. Turn left into Highgate Hill and walk 55 metres to Stop D (Archway Station/Highgate Hill) to board the No. 43 (to Friern Barnet). Disembark at Stop CB (Alexandra Park Road), turn left and walk 35 metres along Colney Hatch Lane to cross at the level crossing. Turn right to walk 5 metres before turning left into Alexandra Park Road and walk 420 metres until having just crossed Grasmere Road where the camera would have filmed this scene looking back in the direction you have just travelled.

Then

Now

Mum waited here for Stan's bus in the opening credits of the first series.

Location 4: The Luxton and District Bus Depot

Series One, Episode One: *The Early Shift*

Omnibus House, Lordship Lane, Wood Green, London, N22 5JY.

This location was to appear frequently throughout the first five series of *On the Buses* and was first seen in the first episode of Series One called *The Early Shift*. We first see Stan in semi-darkness cycle into the depot turning off of Lordship Lane (6 minutes 18 seconds into the episode). This was an actual active bus depot being used by the Eastern National Bus Company at that time but sadly, as you will see from the photographs, the depot has long since been demolished and precisely where the depot stood there now stands a multi-storey block of flats called Omnibus House (obviously in memory of the depot).

How to get there: The most direct route to this location is via tube from King's Cross/St Pancras Station on the Piccadilly Line heading northbound to Wood Green. Exit Wood Green Tube Station and turn left onto Lordship Lane and walk 50 metres. Directly across the road stands Omnibus House.

By bus the most direct route is from Stop J on Tenison Way directly outside Waterloo Station aboard the No. 243 (to Wood Green Station). Disembark at Stop E (Redvers Road), stopping directly outside Omnibus House – the site of the old bus depot.

Then

Now

Omnibus House today where the Wood Green bus depot once stood.

Location 5: The Race to the Rear of the Depot

Series One, Episode One: *The Early Shift*

Lordship Lane, Wood Green, London, N22 5JN.

Later in the first episode, *The Early Shift*, we see Stan, Jack and George run down Lordship Lane and up an alley as they try to prevent a bus breaking the picket line, which is about to exit the rear of the depot (19 minutes 33 seconds into the episode). Of course, this alley which was to the left of the depot entrance, no longer exists but across the road the row of houses are still present and the houses directly in shot are 708 and 706 Lordship Lane with an alley up the side of 708 the giveaway to this location. Aside from cosmetic changes to these houses such as a different arrangement of their chimney stacks, double-glazed windows and new doors being added to the houses, plus a post box standing outside the properties, they remain much the same. The alleyway has now been replaced by an entrance into a car park serving Omnibus House and a Mecca Bingo Club.

How to get there: The most direct route to this location is via tube from King's Cross/St Pancras Station on the Piccadilly Line heading northbound to Wood Green. Exit Wood Green Tube Station and turn left onto Lordship Lane and walk 65 metres. Cross here to the entrance to the car park. Directly across the road stands 708 Lordship Lane.

By bus the most direct route is from Stop J on Tenison Way directly outside Waterloo Station aboard the No. 243 (to Wood Green Station). Disembark at Stop E (Redvers Road). Turn right and walk 10 metres before turning right to cross Lordship Lane to reach the entrance to the car park. Directly across the road stands 708 Lordship Lane.

Then

Now

The view seen down the alleyway across Lordship Lane.

Locations 6 and 7: Public Toilets and Sophie Clothes Shop used by Iris

Series One, Episode Two: *The New Conductor*

Bush Hill Gardens, Village Road, Enfield, London, EN1 2HA.

In the second episode of Series One, *The New Conductor*, Stan's bus waits outside a public park, containing toilets, for his new clippie Iris and she finally exits giving him the thumbs up (7 minutes 38 seconds into the episode) but that isn't the end of the delay to Stan's journey. Iris runs across the road and looks in the window of a ladies' clothes shop called Sophie before entering. Today, the park, known as Bush Hill Gardens in Enfield, remains virtually unchanged aside from the public toilets. Although the curved metal arched gateway marked with the word 'LADIES' remain, the steps leading down into the underground toilets and the toilets themselves no longer exist and there is no trace of them ever being there. The row of shops opposite the park is on Bush Hill Parade with Sophie's shop having long since closed for business, and where that shop stood now is a barber shop – the configuration of windows above the shops, the door alongside leading to a flat, and judging where Stan's bus parked, lead me to the identification of this location.

How to get there: The most direct route to this location is via train from King's Cross Station aboard a Great Northern service to Winchmore Hill. Exit Winchmore Hill Station and turn right onto Station Road and walk around 500 metres onto Green Lanes. From Stop R board the No. 329 bus heading northbound and disembark at Stop W (Bush Hill Road) on Village Road. Walk 50 metres south in the direction you have just travelled to arrive at the location.

By bus the most direct route is from Stop G on Copenhagen Street/York Way (the street that runs directly north on the east side of King's Cross Station) aboard the No. 390. Disembark at Stop J (Wharfdale Road) and change at this stop for the No. 259 bus to Edmonton Green Station. Change here and from Stop R at Edmonton Green Station board the W8 bus (to Chase Farm Hospital) and disembark at Stop W (Bush Hill Road) on Village Road and walk 50 metres south in the direction you have just travelled to arrive at the location.

Then

Now

Note that there is now no trace of the underground toilets but the distinctive arched gates remain.

Then

Now

**H's Barbers was formerly the clothes store called
Sophie that Iris visited.**

Location 8: Olive Feels Unwell

Series One, Episode Three: *Olive Takes a Trip*

Palace Gates Road, Wood Green, London, N22 7BW.

The third episode of Series One, called *Olive Takes a Trip*, sees Stan's bus about to come to a stop (15 minutes 45 seconds into the episode). His sister and trainee clippie is unwell and gets off the bus to tell Stan, where a row of distinctive three-storey houses in the background can be seen to the left of the bus. To the right there is an alleyway at the end of a row of houses. This scene was filmed on Palace Gates Road in Wood Green and today the distinctive houses remain unchanged though the alleyway has gone, with a brick wall now in place here.

How to get there: The most direct route to this location is via train from London King's Cross Station aboard a Great Northern service to Finsbury Park Station. Change here for another Great Northern service to Alexandra Palace Station. Exit Alexandra Palace Station at the Bedford Road exit, turning left to walk 120 metres before turning left into Palace Gates Road. Walk 130 metres before crossing the road, with a brick wall to your right. Across the road you will see the distinctive three-storey houses seen in the episode.

Then

Now

The houses on the right remain unchanged but on the right the alley no longer remains.

Location 9: Olive's Illness Continues

Series One, Episode Three: *Olive Takes a Trip*

Palace Gates Road, Wood Green, London, N22 7BW.

Later in *Olive Takes a Trip*, her travel sickness continues and she rings the bell continuously to stop the bus as it travels up an inclining road (16 minutes 24 seconds into the episode). This scene was filmed about 60 metres further west along Palace Gates Road from the earlier scene in the episode with the bus stopping outside No. 63. The location can be pinpointed by the unusual red brickwork intermingled with occasional white brickwork around the windows at this property, seen when Stan gets out of the bus.

How to get there: The most direct route to this location is via train from London King's Cross Station aboard a Great Northern service to Finsbury Park Station. Change here for another Great Northern service to Alexandra Palace Station. Exit Alexandra Palace Station at the Bedford Road exit, turning left to walk 120 metres before turning left into Palace Gates Road. Walk 190 metres until adjacent to No. 63 Palace Gates Road that is seen in the scene.

Then

Now

Note the parade of shops in the background remain as they were in the episode.

Then

Now

The red-bricked house can be seen in the background during this scene.

Location 10: Stan Ticks off Clippie

Series One, Episode Five: *The New Inspector*

Perth Road, Wood Green, London, N22 5PX.

This location is seen in the fifth episode of Series One, called *The New Inspector*, when a bus pulls up at a bus stop. The scene that follows sees Stan, in his new role as inspector, get off the bus and berate Betty – a clippie who is on friendly terms with the depot manager. This scene (15 minutes 55 seconds into the episode) was filmed on Perth Road in Wood Green just under a half a mile east of the bus depot in Lordship Lane. The location is on the opposite side of the road to No. 19 Perth Road and the entrance to Leith Road is seen in the episode as is a small tree at the end of that road. The park where the bus stops was also a big help in tracking the location down. Today the location has a more leafy appearance.

How to get there: The most direct route to this location is via tube from King's Cross/St Pancras Station on the Piccadilly Line heading northbound to Wood Green. Exit Wood Green Tube Station and turn left onto Lordship Lane and walk 700 metres until reaching the junction with Perth Road. Turn left onto Perth Road and walk 60 metres to the location on the right (across the road from No. 19 Perth Road).

By bus the most direct route is from Stop J on Tenison Way directly outside Waterloo Station aboard the No. 243 (to Wood Green Station). Disembark at Stop NS (Perth Road) on Lordship Lane. Cross the road and walk east for 50 metres and turn left onto Perth Road and a further 60 metres walk brings you to the location (across the road from No. 19 Perth Road).

Then

Now

The bus travels towards the camera to stop here before Stan ticks off Betty.

Location 11: Stan Suffers Bus Stop Frustration

Series One, Episode Five: *The New Inspector*

Perth Road, Wood Green, London, N22 5PY.

The Series One episode, *The New Inspector*, sees Stan waiting at a bus stop (16 minutes 31 seconds into the episode) and he puts out his hand to stop an approaching bus, but to his bemusement it passes him by without stopping. He then hurriedly scribbles down the offending bus on his clipboard. This location (like the previous one) was filmed on Perth Road in Wood Green but further eastwards and directly outside the gate of No. 27 Perth Road. The park opposite was a big clue as was the entrance to Leith Road. The tree seen there in that episode is still there but obviously has grown somewhat. Also the telegraph pole is also present today as it was in the episode.

How to get there: The most direct route to this location is via tube from King's Cross/St Pancras Station on the Piccadilly Line heading northbound to Wood Green. Exit Wood Green Tube Station and turn left onto Lordship Lane and walk 700 metres until reaching the junction with Perth Road. Turn left onto Perth Road and walk 100 metres to the location on the left directly outside No. 27 Perth Road.

By bus the most direct route is from Stop J on Tenison Way directly outside Waterloo Station aboard the No. 243 (to Wood Green Station). Disembark at Stop NS (Perth Road) on Lordship Lane. Cross the road and walk east for 50 metres and turn left onto Perth Road and a further 100 metres walk brings you to the location directly outside No. 27 Perth Road.

Then

Now

Stan waits at a bus stop but the bus passes him by without stopping.

Location 12: Stan's Foot Traps in Bus Door

Series One, Episode Five: *The New Inspector*

Lavender Hill, Enfield, London, EN2 0QU.

Once more in the Series One episode, *The New Inspector*, Stan waits at a bus stop (17 minutes 4 seconds into the episode) and when the bus stops and he goes to board, the door opens and quickly closes again trapping his foot in the door before driving off, leaving Stan to write down another report. This location was one of the easiest to find as you can clearly see a sign post for Gordon Hill Railway Station in the background. It can be pinpointed to great detail as well as Stan stands next to a telegraph pole which still stands there today directly outside a small Co-op store, immediately to the right on exiting the railway station's car park on Lavender Hill.

How to get there: The most direct route to this location is via tube from London Euston on the Victoria Line heading northbound to Highbury and Islington. Change at Highbury and Islington for a Great Northern train service to Gordon Hill Station. Exit Gordon Hill Station through the car park and onto Lavender Hill. Turn right and after a 10 metre walk you will find the telegraph pole that Stan stood beside.

By bus the most direct route is from Stop G on York Way (the street that runs directly north on the eastside of King's Cross Station) aboard the No. 259 bus (to Edmonton Green). Disembark at Edmonton Green Station and from Stop R board the W8 bus to Gordon Hill, disembarking at Stop A (Gordon Hill) which brings you to the exact filming location by the telegraph pole.

Then

Now

Stan looks to board a bus here. The telegraph pole remains to the current day.

Location 13: Stan Regulates Jack

Series One, Episode Five: *The New Inspector*

Alexandra Park Road, Wood Green, London, N10 2AD.

Finally, in *The New Inspector*, Stan is seen waiting at a bus stop with his clipboard as Jack's bus approaches (17 minutes 20 seconds into the episode) and the scene sees Stan regulating Jack to make sure he leaves the stop on time. The bus is seen travelling up a road on a steep incline with three-storey houses on the right sight of the road and to the left two-storey houses. This scene was filmed with Stan standing outside No. 60 Alexandra Park Road as we see the Luxton and District Bus Stop attached to what would have been a lamp post. A more modern lamp post still remains at this location and the three-storey houses are still present and largely unchanged as are the houses on the opposite side of the road.

How to get there: The most direct route to this location is via tube from King's Cross/St Pancras Station on the Northern Line heading northbound to Golders Green. Exit Golders Green Station, turn right and from Stop GU board the No. 102 (to Edmonton Green Bus Station). Disembark at Stop CR (St. Andrew's Church) and turn right and walk 100 metres along Alexandra Park Road until having just crossed Grasmere Road. Cross here to No. 60 where the camera would have filmed this scene looking downhill.

By bus the most direct route is from Stop C outside London Euston Station aboard the No. 390 (to Archway). Disembark at Stop AP (Archway) and turn right to walk five metres. Turn left into Highgate Hill and walk 55 metres to Stop D (Archway Station/Highgate Hill) to board the No. 43 (to Friern Barnet). Disembark at Stop CB (Alexandra Park Road), turn left and walk 35 metres along Colney Hatch Lane to cross at the level crossing. Turn right to walk 5 metres before turning left into Alexandra Park Road and walk 420 metres until having just crossed Grasmere Road. Cross here to No. 60 where the camera would have filmed this scene looking downhill.

Then

Now

Stan stood by the lamp post in this episode which doubled as a bus stop.

Location 14: A Drink at a Country Cottage

Series One, Episode Six: *The Canteen*

The Ridgeway, Enfield, London, EN2 8AP.

In the sixth episode of Series One, *The Canteen*, we see Stan and Jack's bus pull up at a rural bus stop and they get out and cross the road to a row of cottages (8 minutes 59 seconds into the episode). Knocking on the door of one of the cottages an old lady brings them two glasses of water which they hastily drink to counteract the effect of Mrs Sharma's cuisine. This location proved very troublesome to find and is located on the outskirts of London with the cottage used being No, 258 The Ridgeway to the north-west of Enfield. The picket fence seen by the road where the bus pulls up is still present and the cottage next door has a vine creeping up the outside walls and this is still present today. There are cosmetic differences such as an added porch above the front doors but apart from that the cottage is unchanged.

How to get there: The most direct route to this location is via train from London King's Cross Station aboard a Great Northern service to Potters Bar Station. Exit Potters Bar Station and from Stop D board the No. 313 (to Chingford Station) and disembark at the stop for Botany Bay/The Robin Hood (the actual stop Stan's bus stops at) and directly across the road is No. 258 The Ridgeway.

By bus the most direct route is from Stop G on York Way (the street that runs directly north on the eastside of King's Cross Station) aboard the No. 259 bus (to Edmonton Green). Change at Edmonton Green Station and from Stop R board the W8 bus (to Chase Farm Hospital) and disembark at Enfield Town Station. From Stop N board the No. 313 bus (to Potters Bar Station) and disembark at the stop for Botany Bay/The Robin Hood and walk 100 metres north to the location.

Then

Now

The cottage visited by Stan and Jack is today masked by a small tree.

Location 15: Another Drink from the Radiator

Series One, Episode Six: *The Canteen*

The Ridgeway, Enfield, London, EN2 8AN.

Also in the episode, *The Canteen*, Stan and Jack's bus is parked on a country lane and the two thirsty busmen use a hose and feed it into the bus's radiator (9 minutes 30 seconds into the episode). Such is their need for a drink they syphon water from the radiator but soon realise their mistake, spitting out the foul-tasting water. This location is around a third of a mile to the north on The Ridgeway of the previous location and was filmed by the entrance to the Holly Hill Farm. By this entrance is a tree with a gate in the background and a hedge running through the field and all of these are present in the episode.

How to get there: The most direct route to this location is via train from London King's Cross Station aboard a Great Northern service to Potters Bar Station. Exit Potters Bar Station and from Stop D board the No. 313 (to Chingford Station) and disembark at the stop for Windrush. Walk 75 metres to the entrance road to Holly Hill Farm with a tree on the corner.

By bus the most direct route is from Stop G on York Way (the street that runs directly north on the eastside of King's Cross Station) aboard the No. 259 bus (to Edmonton Green). Change at Edmonton Green Station and from Stop R board the W8 bus (to Chase Farm Hospital) and disembark at Enfield Town Station. From Stop N board the No. 313 bus (to Potters Bar Station) and disembark at the stop for Windrush and cross the road, walk 60 metres back in the direction the bus has travelled to the entrance road to Holly Hill Farm with a tree on the corner.

Then

Now

Stan's bus was parked here and the tree can be seen in the background as can the fence and the row of hedges running through the field.

Location 16: Stan Shopping on Duty

Series Two, Episode One: *Family Flu*

Harrow Road, Wembley, London, HA9 6PG.

The first episode in Series Two, called *Family Flu*, sees Stan shopping whilst on duty. He is to exit Moss Stores (1 minute 7 seconds into the episode) with two bags of shopping as Jack waits impatiently by the bus. This scene was filmed on Harrow Road in Wembley around a mile to the south-west of the LWT studios. The Moss Stores shop, of course, has long since ceased trading but it was located where a Royal Chicken takeaway shop now stands and this can be deduced accurately when we see the bus pull away and a block of flats opposite come into sight – using that building's window configuration leads me to be able to pinpoint the shop location.

How to get there: The most direct route to this location is via train from London Euston Station aboard a London Overground service to Stonebridge Park Station. Exit Stonebridge Park Station, turning right on Argenta Way. After 40 metres turn left onto North Circular Road and then after 100 metres turn left onto Harrow Road. Cross Harrow Road and walk a further 100 metres to 20 Harrow Road – the filming location at Royal Chicken takeaway shop.

By bus the most direct route is from Stop H outside London Euston Station aboard the No. 18 bus (to Sudbury). Disembark at Stop C (Monks Park) on Harrow Road and walk 20 metres back in the direction you have just travelled and cross at the level crossing, turn right and walk 80 metres to the filming location at 20 Harrow Road – the Royal Chicken takeaway shop.

Then

Now

Formerly the Moss Stores where Stan does his shopping for the family.

Location 17: Stan Arrives Home

Series Two, Episode One: *Family Flu*

Selwyn Road, Brent, London, NW10 8QY.

Also in Series Two, Episode One, *Family Flu*, Stan can be seen crossing a road with his shopping and walking to the front gate of his house (5 minutes 3 seconds into the episode). As he fumbles for his front door key you can clearly see No. 34 on the door so we can safely say this was No. 34 Selwyn Road. The big clue to this location, of course, was the power station that looms large in the background. We see this location again from a different angle (23 minutes 34 seconds into the same episode) when the family board a taxi bound for a visit to Aunt Maud and as it departs with Jack waving them off you can see a tree outside the house that still remains there today.

How to get there: The most direct route to this location is via bus from London Euston Station from Stop H aboard the No. 18 bus (to Sudbury). Disembark at Stop V (Knatchbull Road) on Craven Park Road and walk north 100 metres. Turn right onto Craven Park and then after 10 metres turn left onto Bruce Road and walk for 180 metres before turning right onto Hazeldean Road. Finally, after 200 metres take a slight left turn onto Selwyn Road and after 55 metres you will find No. 34 on your right.

Then

Now

The power station remains although the large rotund chimneys have gone.

Then

Now

The taxi pulls away roughly from where the tree on the right stands today.

Location 18: The FORCO Launderette

Series Two, Episode One: *Family Flu*

Church Lane, West Hendon, London, NW9 8SN.

Another location seen in *Family Flu* comes when Stan exits a launderette called FORCO carrying a bag of washing but is challenged by a housewife (18 minutes 50 seconds into the episode). This scene was tricky to pinpoint but the clues were the doorway next to the launderette which is still there today, the same window configuration of the launderette as is today, distinctive brickwork and the shopping parade opposite having distinguishing features, although the wooden posts across the pavement present today were not a feature in 1969. Today a launderette is still located on site at No. 226 Church Lane and it is roughly a mile to the north-east of the old LWT studios.

How to get there: The most direct route to this location is via tube from King's Cross/St Pancras Station on the Metropolitan Line heading northbound to Wembley Park Tube Station. Exit Wembley Park Tube Station and from Stop N directly outside board the No. 83 bus. Disembark at Stop BE (Lavender Avenue) and walk 95 metres north and cross at the level crossing. On your right you will see the launderette at No. 226 Church Lane.

By bus the most direct route is from Stop H outside London Euston Station aboard the No. 18 bus to Sudbury. Disembark at Stop V (Ladbroke Grove/Kilburn Lane) and from this stop board the No. 28 bus to Kensal Rise, disembarking at Stop KR at Kensal Rise Station. From this stop board the No. 302 bus to Mill Hill Broadway, disembarking at Stop BE (Lavender Avenue) and walk 95 metres north. Cross at the level crossing and on your right you will see the launderette at No. 226 Church Lane.

Then

Now

**The launderette remains very much the same
approaching 50 years later.**

Location 19: Arthur Receives Tools

Series Two, Episode Two: *The Used Combination*

East Lane, Wembley, London, HA0 3NJ.

Arthur waits by a bus stop (12 minutes 19 seconds into the episode, *The Used Combination*). The bus pulls up and Jack hands him tools wrapped up in paper before the bus pulls away with a policeman watching on in interest. This scene was filmed in East Lane, Wembley just under a mile to the east of the LWT Studios. The clues to this location were the hump-backed bridge with a telephone box on it and two small box-shaped houses on the corner of the road behind him. All of these features are still present today and Arthur stood on the pavement outside No. 102 East Lane where a bus stop still stands today.

How to get there: The most direct route to this location is via tube from London Marylebone Station on the Bakerloo Line heading northbound to North Wembley Tube Station. Exit North Wembley Tube Station and turn left onto East Lane, walk 30 metres crossing Harrowdene Road to a level crossing and cross here, turning left and walk 70 metres to the location at the bus stop outside No. 102 East Lane.

By bus the most direct route is from Stop P outside London Marylebone Station aboard the No. 18 bus (to Sudbury). Disembark at Stop J (Sudbury and Harrow Road Station) and from this stop board the No. 245 bus (to Golders Green) disembarking at Stop N (North Wembley) which is the stop Arthur waited at all those years ago.

Then

Now

Arthur stood here and the white house with a public phone box outside remains in the background.

Location 20: Arthur's Motorbike Breaks Down

Series Two, Episode Two: *The Used Combination*

East Lane, Wembley, London, HA0 3LF.

The Used Combination episode sees Arthur's new acquisition – a second-hand motorcycle combination break down 17 minutes 21 seconds into the episode. As Arthur throws his gloves down in frustration we can see a grassy verge with trees to the left and houses in the background. This location was filmed on East Lane on the junction with Oldborough Road and today the location has changed very little, but the tight roads are now heavily occupied by parked cars. The path across the patch of grass remains as do the trees and hedges but I'd say confidently that there were never any toilets there and the toilet sign was put up for filming.

How to get there: The most direct route to this location is via tube from London Marylebone Station on the Bakerloo Line heading northbound to North Wembley Tube Station. Exit North Wembley Tube Station and turn left onto East Lane, walk 340 metres to a zebra crossing and cross here, turn left and walk 5 metres taking a right-hand turn after. The location is 40 metres walk on your left in a layby by the grassy verge.

By bus the most direct route is from Stop P outside London Marylebone Station aboard the No. 18 bus (to Sudbury). Disembark at Stop J (Sudbury and Harrow Road Station) and from this stop board the No. 245 bus (to Golders Green) disembarking at Stop M (Sudbury Court) and walk up the path across the grass verge. At its end is the filming location by the layby.

Then

Now

The sidecar came to a halt where the car in the foreground is parked.

Location 21: Bus Towing the Motorbike

Series Two, Episode Two: *The Used Combination*

Oldborough Road, Wembley, London, HA0 3PR.

Stan and Jack come to Arthur's rescue and tow his motorbike with their bus and we see the bus turning a corner with a school in the background (18 minutes 43 seconds into the episode *The Used Combination*) into a street lined by houses. It follows the bus as it carries on down past the turn into Holt Road. The camera would have been filming the bus precisely outside No. 6 Oldborough Road and today the school in the background remains although development work has taken place over the years and we see the tree on the left still there today. This location is 50 metres from where the previous location was filmed.

How to get there: The most direct route to this location is via tube from London Marylebone Station on the Bakerloo Line heading northbound to North Wembley Tube Station. Exit North Wembley Tube Station and turn left onto East Lane, walk 340 metres to a zebra crossing and cross here, turn left and walk 5 metres taking a right-hand turn. Walk 50 metres and turn right at the junction and into Oldborough Road and walk another 50 metres to the gate of No. 6, where the camera would roughly have been positioned for this scene.

By bus the most direct route is from Stop P outside London Marylebone Station aboard the No. 18 bus (to Sudbury). Disembark at Stop J (Sudbury and Harrow Road Station) and from this stop board the No. 245 bus (to Golders Green) disembarking at Stop M (Sudbury Court) and walk up the path across the grass verge. Cross the road directly in front of you and turn right onto Oldborough Road and after a 50 metres walk you will reach the gate to No. 6 at the filming point of the location.

Then

Now

The corner where the bus turns with the motorbike and sidecar in tow.

Location 22: The Handlebars Come Off

Series Two, Episode Two: *The Used Combination*

Holt Road, Wembley, London, HA0 3PY.

In the following scene the handlebars are seen being dragged along behind the bus but the motorbike and sidecar with Arthur, Olive and mum aboard are left stationary in the middle of the road (exactly 19 minutes into the episode). The motorbike is standing outside No. 13 Holt Road and this location can be pinpointed accurately by the house over Arthur's right shoulder. The garage, the distinctive porch above the door, and tree outside No. 15 are all present today and is unique in the street. It can be identified as Holt Road by the exact position and design of the houses at the end of the street in the distance seen in the episode.

How to get there: The most direct route to this location is via tube from London Marylebone Station on the Bakerloo Line heading northbound to North Wembley Tube Station. Exit North Wembley Tube Station and turn left onto East Lane, walk 340 metres to a zebra crossing and cross here, turn left and walk 5 metres taking a right-hand turn. Walk 50 metres and turn right at the junction and into Oldborough Road. Walk 100 metres, turn left into Holt Road and walk 60 metres to No. 13 Holt Road.

By bus the most direct route is from Stop P outside London Marylebone Station aboard the No. 18 bus (to Sudbury). Disembark at Stop J (Sudbury and Harrow Road Station) and from this stop board the No. 245 bus (to Golders Green) disembarking at Stop M (Sudbury Court) and walk up the path across the grass verge. Cross the road directly in front of you and turn right onto Oldborough Road and walk 100 metres, turn left into Holt Road and walk 60 metres to No. 13 Holt Road.

Then

Now

The tree to the left is seen over Arthur's right shoulder as he sits on the stationary motorbike and sidecar.

Location 23: Jack Notices the Bike Has Gone

Series Two, Episode Two: *The Used Combination*

The Fairway, Wembley, London, HA0 3LP.

Once more in *The Used Combination*, after Jack notices the bus is towing only handlebars as it turns a corner he dings on the bell for the bus to stop and disembarks running to the rear of the bus (19 minutes 8 seconds into the episode). When he tells Stan the bike has gone we see a house with a small, black, wrought iron gate and fence in the background and those features thankfully still remain outside No. 41 The Fairway. We can therefore ascertain that the bus was filmed turning left out of Blockley Road into The Fairway where it came to a halt.

How to get there: The most direct route to this location is via tube from London Marylebone Station on the Bakerloo Line heading northbound to North Wembley Tube Station. Exit North Wembley Tube Station and turn left onto East Lane, walk 340 metres to a zebra crossing and cross here, turn left and walk 5 metres taking a right-hand turn. Walk 50 metres and turn left at the junction, after a walk of 80 metres turn right into The Fairway and walk 250 metres to No. 41 The Fairway on your left.

By bus the most direct route is from Stop P outside London Marylebone Station aboard the No. 18 bus (to Sudbury). Disembark at Stop J (Sudbury and Harrow Road Station) and from this stop board the No. 245 bus (to Golders Green) disembarking at Stop M (Sudbury Court) and walk 150 metres back in the direction the bus has just travelled from. Turn right into The Fairway and walk 250 metres to No. 41 The Fairway on your left.

Then

Now

The bus minus the bike it was towing stopped here.

Then

Now

This black wrought iron gate and fence is seen behind Jack when he speaks to Stan.

Location 24: Stan Visits Doreen's House

Series Two, Episode Five: *Late Again*

Twybridge Way, Willesden, London, NW10 0SU.

In the fifth episode of Series Two, *Late Again*, Stan is disappointed to find Jack at his girlfriend Doreen's house. After berating his best friend he leaves (24 minutes 24 seconds into the episode) and walks down the road as the closing credits roll. This location was around a mile to the south-east of LWT's studios at No. 43 Twybridge Way and was pinpointed by the angled row of houses seen at the far end of the street and arched doorways in the houses opposite.

How to get there: The most direct route to this location is via train from London Euston Station aboard a London Overground service to Stonebridge Park Station. Exit Stonebridge Park Station turning right on Argenta Way. After 40 metres turn left onto the North Circular Road and walk for 230 metres. Turn right onto Harrow Road and walk for 110 metres and turn left onto Conduit Way. After a 345 metres walk, turn right onto Twybridge Way and walk for 150 metres to the location at No. 43.

By bus the most direct route is from Stop H outside London Euston Station aboard the No. 18 bus (to Sudbury). Disembark at Stop K (North Circular Road/Brentfield) and cross the road and walk 60 metres before turning right into Conduit Way. After a 345 metres walk, turn right onto Twybridge Way and walk for 150 metres to the location at No. 43.

Then

Now

The view today from No. 43 Twybridge Way.

Location 25: The Cemetery Gates

Series Two, Episode Six: *Bon Voyage*

Lavender Hill Cemetery, 4 Cedar Road, Enfield, London, EN2 0TH.

Perhaps the most iconic location in *On the Buses* first appears in Series Two, Episode Six. In *Bon Voyage*, we see their bus parked outside cemetery gates (10 minutes 36 seconds into the episode) and then seconds later a passing tramp steals Stan's uniform from the unoccupied driver's cab as Stan and Jack sunbathe in the cemetery. The cemetery gates appear again in several more episodes in Series Three and perhaps they were chosen for the secluded nature of the location.

How to get there: The most direct route to this location is via tube from London Euston on the Victoria Line heading northbound to Highbury and Islington. Change at Highbury and Islington for a Great Northern train service to Gordon Hill Station. Exit Gordon Hill Station through the car park and onto Lavender Hill. Cross the road and walk down the adjacent Lavender Gardens for 195 metres before reaching the left-hand gates into Lavender Hill Cemetery.

By bus the most direct route is from Stop G on York Way (the street that runs directly north on the eastside of King's Cross Station) aboard the No. 259 bus (to Edmonton Green). Disembark at Edmonton Green Station and from Stop R board the W8 bus to Gordon Hill disembarking at Stop A (Gordon Hill) and cross the road and walk down the adjacent Lavender Gardens for 195 metres before reaching the left-hand gates into Lavender Hill Cemetery.

Then

Now

These are the cemetery gates seen in the episode and are the left-hand gates which are no longer in use. This can be ascertained by the rusted padlock on the gates.

Location 26: Stan and Jack Sunbathe in the Cemetery

Series Two, Episode Six: *Bon Voyage*

Lavender Hill Cemetery, 4 Cedar Road, Enfield, London, EN2 0TH.

In a bid to get a suntan before their holiday, Stan and Jack sunbathe in the cemetery in *Bon Voyage*. Stripped to their swimming trunks (10 minutes 38 seconds into the episode) the busmen lie on a stretch of grass with a distinctive looking grave in the background, which is set somewhat at an angle in the ground which helped greatly in identifying this location. The scene was filmed close to the gates (now out of use) at Lavender Hill Cemetery and the surrounding headstones remain pretty much unchanged.

How to get there: The most direct route to this location is via tube from London Euston on the Victoria Line heading northbound to Highbury and Islington. Change at Highbury and Islington for a Great Northern train service to Gordon Hill Station. Exit Gordon Hill Station through the car park and onto Lavender Hill. Cross the road and walk down the adjacent Lavender Gardens for 200 metres, before reaching the gates into Lavender Hill Cemetery. Walk 10 metres through the gates and turn left to walk another 10 metres until adjacent to a large tree on your right. Look north-west to a large grave with a border which is not quite level and this is where Stan and Jack sunbathed in front of this grave.

By bus the most direct route is from Stop G on York Way (the street that runs directly north on the eastside of King's Cross Station) aboard the No. 259 bus (to Edmonton Green). Disembark at Edmonton Green Station and from Stop R board the W8 bus to Gordon Hill disembarking at Stop A (Gordon Hill) and cross the road and walk down the adjacent Lavender Gardens for 200 metres. Cross the road and walk 10 metres through the gates and turn left to walk another 10 metres until adjacent to a large tree on your right. Look north-west to a large grave with a border which is not quite level and this is where Stan and Jack sunbathed in front of this grave.

Then

Now

Stan and Jack sunbathed here.

Location 27: Bus picks up the Butler Family and their Toilet

Series Three, Episode Two: *The Cistern*

Station Road, Hendon, London, NW4 4PN.

After purchasing their toilet the family board Jack's bus, despite his reservations, with their shopping and the bus is seen pulling away from the bus stop (15 minutes 10 seconds into the second episode in Series Three, called *The Cistern*). The bus stop is beside a house and across the road in the background the Midland Hotel can be seen. The bus stop remains at this location to this day on Station Road, Hendon but the house beside the bus stop in the episode was the last in the line of houses on the west side of Algernon Road which were demolished to make way for an extension to the M1 motorway. The Sankey shop would have been to the right (out of shot) but has also long since been demolished.

How to get there: The most direct route to this location is via train from London St Pancras Station (Lower Levels) aboard a Thameslink service to Hendon Station. Exit Hendon Station and turn right. After ten metres turn right onto Station Road and cross at the level crossing. Turn left and walk 35 metres to the bus stop used by the Butler family in the episode.

By bus the most direct route is from Stop Q on Marylebone Road aboard the No. 113 bus (to Edgeware Station). Disembark at Stop H (Hendon War Memorial) and continue along Watford Way, in the direction the bus was travelling, for 40 metres. Turn left onto Station Road and walk for 800 metres to the bus stop used by the Butler family in the episode shortly after passing the Midland Hotel on your right-hand side.

Then

Now

The bus stop where Stan and Arthur board Jack's bus with their new toilet.

Location 28: Blakey at a Bus Stop

Series Three, Episode Two: *The Cistern*

Station Road, Hendon, London, NW4 3SS.

Later on in *The Cistern* episode we see Blakey standing by a bus stop (15 minutes 16 seconds into the episode) looking at his clipboard as Stan's bus approaches. Behind him a residential small block of flats can just be seen behind a line of trees and the distinctive looking houses opposite on a road with a slight incline identifies this as Station Road in Hendon. The residential flats behind him are now the High Mount private properties and Blakey was standing directly in line with No. 55 Station Road across the road. This location is around 100 metres northeast of the Sankey shop's location used in this episode.

How to get there: The most direct route to this location is via train from London St Pancras Station (Lower Levels) aboard a Thameslink service to Hendon Station. Exit Hendon Station and turn right. After ten metres turn right onto Station Road and cross at the level crossing. Turn left and walk 245 metres up Station Road and a few steps past a small flight of steps leading to 1 to 10 High Mount and you will have reached the filming location.

By bus the most direct route is from Stop Q on Marylebone Road aboard the No. 113 bus (to Edgeware Station). Disembark at Stop H (Hendon War Memorial) and continue along Watford Way, in the direction the bus was travelling, for 40 metres. Turn left onto Station Road and walk for 620 metres prior to reaching a small flight of stairs leading to 1 to 10 High Mount and you will have reached the filming location.

Then

Now

Blakey stood here with his clipboard.

Location 29: Terry's Florist Shop

Series Three, Episode Three: *The Inspector's Niece*

Horsenden Lane North, Greenford, London, UB6 7QH.

The third episode in Series Three, *The Inspector's Niece*, sees Stan and Jack vying for the affections of Sally, a trainee clippie. Stan's bus pulls up outside a row of shops (16 minutes 42 seconds into the episode) and Jack takes the opportunity to rush to a florist shop called Terry's to buy a bunch of flowers for Sally. However, Stan drives off as Jack rushes back to the bus, leaving the conductor seething. This row of shops proved very difficult to find, but once located the clues were still there. Terry's had black brickwork at its base and this is still present at No. 94 which is now 1st Class Training – a driving instructor's shop. Across the road from the row of shops, as the bus pulls away, is a street with a tree on one side of the road and houses on the other with distinguishing adornments that are still present to this day, although an extra property has been built at the end of this row of houses.

How to get there: The most direct route to this location is via tube from Kings Cross/London St Pancras Station on the Metropolitan Line heading northbound to Harrow-on-the-Hill Station. Exit Harrow-on-the-Hill Station and turn left to walk 50 metres to Harrow Bus Station. From Stop C board the H17 (to Wembley Central) and disembark at Stop S (Ridding Lane). Cross Whitton Avenue East and turn left to walk 60 metres before turning right into Melville Avenue. Walk 350 metres until adjacent with the row of shops, with the scene roughly being shot by the lamp post near the telephone box.

By bus the most direct route is from Stop H outside London Euston Station aboard the No.18 bus (to Sudbury and Harrow Station). Disembark at Stop F (Bridgewater Road), turn right and walk 40 metres along Harrow Road before turning left into Bridgewater Road. Walk 380 metres before turning right into Whitton Avenue East to cross here and turn right to walk a further 15 metres to Stop W and board either the H17 (to Harrow) or the No. 487 (to South Harrow), disembarking at Stop T (Ridding Lane). Turn left and walk 40 metres before turning right into Melville Avenue. Walk 350 metres until adjacent with the row of shops, with the scene roughly being shot by the lamp post near the telephone box.

Then

Now

The telephone box remains in a newer design as does the wide pavement.

Then

Now

Note the house extension at the end of Robin Hood Way.

Location 30: Stan and Arthur Enter via the Rear Door

Series Three, Episode Two: *The Cistern*

Station Road, Hendon, London, NW4 3SS.

After being asked to remove their new toilet from Jack's bus by the inspector in *The Cistern*, Stan and Arthur sneak aboard the bus via the emergency exit door at the rear (17 minutes 44 seconds into the episode). The bus is parked on a downhill stretch of a residential road with a side road off to the right and four-storey residential housing ahead of the bus on the right as we look. This was filmed at the same location as the previous entry with the camera looking south down Station Road and today very little has changed with this filming location.

How to get there: The most direct route to this location is via train from London St Pancras Station (Lower Levels) aboard a Thameslink service to Hendon Station. Exit Hendon Station and turn right and after ten metres turn right onto Station Road and cross at the level crossing. Turn left and walk 245 metres up Station Road and a few steps past a small flight of stairs leading to 1 to 10 High Mount and you will have reached the filming location when turning to look back down the road you have just travelled up for the correct angle.

By bus the most direct route is from Stop Q on Marylebone Road aboard the No. 113 bus (to Edgware Station). Disembark at Stop H (Hendon War Memorial) and continue along Watford Way in the direction the bus was travelling for 40 metres. Turn left onto Station Road and walk for 620 metres prior to reaching a small flight of stairs leading to 1 to 10 High Mount and turn to look west for the filming location.

Then

Now

**Stan and Arthur bundle their new toilet aboard Jack's
bus via the rear emergency door.**

Location 31: Stan Pays a Gas Bill

Series Three, Episode Seven: *Mum's Last Fling*

Olympic Way, Wembley, London, HA9 0UU.

Stan is forced into paying a bill at the North Thames Gas Board whilst on duty in the seventh episode of Series Three, called *Mum's Last Fling* (16 minutes 38 seconds into the episode). He parks his bus on a road on a slight decline by a row of parking meters and rushes into a multi-storey building to pay his bill. This building is now the Michaela Community College on Olympic Way and a lot has changed since this episode was filmed here. Structurally, the building is the same but the road outside has been lowered by around two metres and is no longer a through road. It has been pedestrianised and is only open to service vehicles and to gain access to the building a flight of steps from ground level lead up to it. This location was very convenient for filming with it being 200 metres away from the studios and if you look carefully in the Series Six episode, *The Prize*, you see the building in the background as Blakey attempts to sell raffle tickets to Stan and Jack.

How to get there: The most direct route to this location is via tube from either King's Cross/St Pancras Station on the Metropolitan Line or from Waterloo on the Jubilee Line, both heading northbound to Wembley Park. Exit Wembley Park Tube Station and turn left, walking 5 metres to a level crossing. Cross and turn right and walk 60 metres before turning left onto Olympic Way. After walking 40 metres you will find the building seen in the episode on your left-hand side.

By bus the most direct route is from Stop H at London Euston Station aboard the No. 18 bus (to Sudbury). Change at Wembley Central Station and board the No. 223 (to Harrow) from Stop CM and disembark at Stop M (Wembley Park) on Bridge Road. Walk 50 metres (in the direction the bus has just brought you) and cross at the level crossing. Turn right and walk 60 metres before turning left onto Olympic Way. After walking 40 metres you will find the building seen in the episode on your left-hand side.

Then

Now

The North Thames Gas Board building.

Location 32: Stan's Bus Hits a Low-Level Bridge

Series Three, Episode Eight: *Radio Control*

North Way, Uxbridge, London, UX10 9NG.

In the eighth episode of Series Three, *Radio Control*, Stan is ordered to take a diversion into an area he doesn't know by Inspector Blake before we see a roadside sign being put up (21 minutes 9 seconds into the episode) and the bus ends up crashing into a low-level bridge. This location has remained largely unchanged, with the extremely narrow nature of the bridge and surrounding features making it not too difficult to find. The only discernible difference being an addition of traffic lights on the entrance to the bridge and cosmetic renovations to houses lining the road. This location did mean around a five-mile journey to the west of LWT studios for the cast, crew and equipment to film this scene.

How to get there: The most direct route to this location is via tube from King's Cross/St Pancras Station on the Metropolitan Line heading northbound to Uxbridge Underground Station. Exit Uxbridge Underground Station and from Stop N board the U2 bus (to Brunel University Kingston Lane) and disembark at the Honey Hill (undesignated) stop. Turn left and walk 150 metres, then turn right into North Way and the bridge is within view.

By bus the most direct route is from Stop H at London Euston Station aboard the No. 30 bus (to Marble Arch). Disembark at Marble Arch Station and from Stop P board the No. 94 (to Acton Green) or the No. 148 (to Shepherd's Bush) and disembark at Shepherd's Bush Station. From Stop C at Shepherd's Bush Station board the No. 607 bus (to Uxbridge) and disembark at the Park Road/Civic Centre (undesignated) stop. Turn right and walk 330 metres along Park Road and cross the road and take a slight right-hand turn on to Honeycroft Hill. Walk for 380 metres and turn left onto North Way and the bridge is within view.

Then

Now

The low-level bridge which Stan crashes his bus into.

Then

Now

Stan gets out of his cab to survey the damage and this is how the location looks today.

Location 33: Arthur's Smoking Motorcycle

Series Three, Episode Twelve: *The Squeeze*

Dean Court, Wembley, London, HA0 3PX.

Stan and Jack take Inspector Blake out for a trial run in Arthur's motorbike and sidecar as he shows an interest in purchasing it in the twelfth episode of Series Three, *The Squeeze*. However, not long into the journey, smoke billows out of the bike as it travels down a street lined by distinctive houses (19 minutes 52 seconds into the episode). The bike can be seen passing No. 4 and No. 6 Dean Court in Wembley and this is identifiable by the grass-covered traffic island in the turn out of the road, which is just visible as the bike turns out of Dean Court and into Holt Road and where I believe the camera would have filmed this scene from.

How to get there: The most direct route to this location is via tube from London Marylebone Station on the Bakerloo Line heading northbound to North Wembley Tube Station. Exit North Wembley Tube Station and turn left onto East Lane, walk 340 metres to a zebra crossing and cross here, turn left and walk 5 metres taking a right-hand turn. Walk 50 metres and turn left at the junction and after a walk of 80 metres turn right into The Fairway and walk 100 metres and at the next junction turn right into Holt Road. Walk 80 metres to the grass-covered traffic island where this scene was filmed from.

By bus the most direct route is from Stop P outside London Marylebone Station aboard the No. 18 bus (to Sudbury). Disembark at Stop J (Sudbury and Harrow Road Station) and from this stop board the No. 245 bus (to Golders Green) disembarking at Stop M (Sudbury Court) and walk 150 metres back in the direction the bus has just travelled from. Turn right into The Fairway and walk 100 metres and at the next junction turn right into Holt Road. Walk 80 metres to the grass-covered traffic island where this scene was filmed from.

Then

Now

The smoking motorbike and sidecar rounds this corner.

Location 34: Sawdust on Fire

Series Three, Episode Twelve: *The Squeeze*

Holt Road, Wembley, London, HA0 3PS.

When the motorbike and sidecar carrying Stan, Jack and Blakey comes to a stop as it smokes badly in *The Squeeze*, Jack leaps off the bike and in a panic tells Stan he thinks the sawdust put in the gearbox to ensure smoother running has caught fire. This scene (20 minutes 3 seconds into the episode) was filmed directly outside No. 14 Holt Road with 1 Dean Court across the road in the background. The area has not changed at all aside from a few properties having minor renovations and unusually it would seem that the whole motorbike and sidecar trial run scenes were filmed in the order they appear in the episode.

How to get there: The most direct route to this location is via tube from London Marylebone Station on the Bakerloo Line heading northbound to North Wembley Tube Station. Exit North Wembley Tube Station and turn left onto East Lane, walk 340 metres to a zebra crossing and cross here, turn left and walk 5 metres taking a right-hand turn. Walk 50 metres and turn left at the junction and after a walk of 80 metres turn right into The Fairway and walk 100 metres and at the next junction turn right into Holt Road. Walk 70 metres to No.14 Holt Road where this scene was filmed.

By bus the most direct route is from Stop P outside London Marylebone Station aboard the No. 18 bus (to Sudbury). Disembark at Stop J (Sudbury and Harrow Road Station) and from this stop board the No. 245 bus (to Golders Green) disembarking at Stop M (Sudbury Court) and walk 150 metres back in the direction the bus has just travelled from. Turn right into The Fairway and walk 100 metres and at the next junction turn right into Holt Road. Walk 70 metres to No. 14 Holt Road where this scene was filmed.

Then

Now

The sidecar stops here with the sawdust in the gearbox on fire.

Location 35: The Missing Sidecar

Series Three, Episode Twelve: *The Squeeze*

Campden Crescent, Wembley, London, HA0 3JQ.

Stan and Jack are seen riding the motorbike as it turns a right-hand bend into another street but the sidecar is missing (20 minutes 32 seconds into *The Squeeze*) and it comes to a halt with Stan and Jack running back up the road to search for it. This would have been filmed from the pavement outside No. 6 Campden Crescent as Stan and Jack exit Stapenhill Road and turn right into Campden Crescent. The distinctive house on the corner of the street that they exit is the clue, with the striking white and black façade, and the slight decline of the road was also a help in pinpointing this filming location.

How to get there: The most direct route to this location is via tube from London Marylebone Station on the Bakerloo Line heading northbound to North Wembley Tube Station. Exit North Wembley Tube Station and turn left onto East Lane, walk 340 metres to a zebra crossing and cross here, turn left and walk 5 metres taking a right-hand turn. Walk 50 metres and turn left at the junction and after a walk of 80 metres turn right into The Fairway and walk 100 metres and at the next junction turn left into Campden Crescent. Walk 60 metres to No. 6 Campden Crescent where this scene was filmed.

By bus the most direct route is from Stop P outside London Marylebone Station aboard the No. 18 bus (to Sudbury). Disembark at Stop J (Sudbury and Harrow Road Station) and from this stop board the No. 245 bus (to Golders Green) disembarking at Stop M (Sudbury Court) and walk 150 metres back in the direction the bus has just travelled from. Turn right into The Fairway and walk 100 metres and at the next junction turn left into Campden Crescent. Walk 60 metres to No. 6 Campden Crescent where this scene was filmed.

Then

Now

The house on the corner in centre of shot remains much unchanged today.

Location 36: The Sidecar is Found

Series Three, Episode Twelve: *The Squeeze*

The Fairway, Wembley, London, HA0 3LJ.

Finally, in *The Squeeze*, we see the detached sidecar (20 minutes 48 seconds into the episode) with Blakey trapped inside sitting in the middle of a suburban road. The clue to this location is the house in the background with ornate decorations on its garden wall which still remain there to this day and are unique to this street. Using that house as a landmark the sidecar would have stood in the road directly outside No. 12 The Fairway. This location proved troublesome to track down as both garages in shot and houses have undergone great renovations and at least three properties have had extensions added.

How to get there: The most direct route to this location is via tube from London Marylebone Station on the Bakerloo Line heading northbound to North Wembley Tube Station. Exit North Wembley Tube Station and turn left onto East Lane, walk 340 metres to a zebra crossing and cross here, turn left and walk 5 metres taking a right-hand turn. Walk 50 metres and turn left at the junction and after a walk of 80 metres turn right into The Fairway and walk 120 metres until directly outside No. 12 The Fairway with the sidecar directly outside this property.

By bus the most direct route is from Stop P outside London Marylebone Station aboard the No. 18 bus (to Sudbury). Disembark at Stop J (Sudbury and Harrow Road Station) and from this stop board the No. 245 bus (to Golders Green) disembarking at Stop L (Pasture Road). Turn right and walk 10 metres before turning left into Pasture Road. Walk 130 metres and turn right into Stapenhill Road and walk 100 metres to No. 12 where this location was filmed.

Then

Now

The sidecar with Blakey trapped inside stood in the road here.

Then

Now

The backdrop seen when Jack suggests that Stan breaks the glass.

Then

Now

The view behind Stan when he refuses to spoil the moment. Note the house has undergone an extension.

Location 37: The Butlers Prepare to Visit Aunt Maud

Series Four, Episode One: *Nowhere To Go*

Selwyn Road, Brent, London, NW10 8QX.

The first episode of Series Four, called *Nowhere To Go*, sees Arthur, Olive and Mum board the motorbike and sidecar which is parked outside their house before departing on a visit to Aunt Maud with Stan and Jack waving them off (20 minutes 31 seconds into the episode). The red-bricked houses with trees lining the street and the tight left-hand curve in the road seen later in the scene helped identify this location as Selwyn Road as used in earlier and later episodes. However, unlike in *Family Flu* in Series Two, which used No. 34, this time the Butler house was located at No. 3 Selwyn Road around 40 metres south on the opposite side of the road. We see this location again in the fifth episode of Series Four, *Christmas Duty*, as Arthur, Olive and Mum (16 minutes into the episode) prepare to pick Stan up from the depot.

How to get there: The most direct route to this location is via bus from London Euston Station from Stop H aboard the No. 18 bus (to Sudbury). Disembark at Stop V (Knatchbull Road) on Craven Park Road and walk north 100 metres, turn right onto Craven Park and then after 10 metres turn left onto Bruce Road and walk for 180 metres before turning right onto Hazeldean Road. Finally, after 200 metres, take a slight left turn onto Selwyn Road and after 10 metres you will find No. 3 on your left.

Then

Now

Stan stood on the pavement here waving goodbye to the family alongside Jack.

Location 38: The Sidecar Mounts a Pavement

Series Four, Episode Five: *Christmas Duty*

Selwyn Road, Brent, London, NW10 8QY.

With Arthur too drunk to drive it is left up to Olive (as a learner) to take the family to the bus depot to pick up Stan. The motorbike and sidecar departs from outside the Butler house at No. 3 Selwyn Road and swerves across the road to mount the pavement (16 minutes 44 seconds into the episode) rounding a tree outside No. 4 Selwyn Road. Today the tree remains to this day but has grown somewhat in size and the lamp post a few metres away also remains in place with the properties lining the road largely unchanged.

How to get there: The most direct route to this location is via bus from London Euston Station from Stop H aboard the No. 18 bus (to Sudbury). Disembark at Stop V (Knatchbull Road) on Craven Park Road and walk north 100 metres, turn right onto Craven Park and then after 10 metres turn left onto Bruce Road and walk for 180 metres before turning right onto Hazeldean Road. Finally, after 200 metres take a slight left turn onto Selwyn Road and after 10 metres you will find No. 3 on your left. Turn around to face the direction you have travelled from and on the left side of the road 10 metres ahead is the tree the motorbike and sidecar rounds.

Then

Now

**Olive steers the motorbike and sidecar
precariously around this tree.**

Location 39: Picking up Stan

Series Four, Episode Five: *Christmas Duty*

Redvers Road, Wood Green, London, N22 6EQ.

The motorbike and sidecar, with Olive driving, and Arthur and Mum as passengers, approaches the rear of the bus depot (17 minutes 13 seconds into the episode, *Christmas Duty*). At the bottom of the street we see a turret-like structure on the end house and this and the proximity of the bus depot helped identify this filming location as Redvers Road. This location is seen again in the later Series Four episode, *Safety First*, and the Series Five episode, *Lost Property*. Today Redvers Road has undergone much change since *On the Buses* was filmed here. Only the houses at the Moselle Avenue end of Redvers Road remain and the rest of the street has had a range of new houses built on either side of the road, whilst the rear of a large shopping complex is now present at the Lordship Road end of the road.

How to get there: The most direct route to this location is via tube from King's Cross/St Pancras Station on the Piccadilly Line heading northbound to Wood Green. Exit Wood Green Tube Station and turn left onto Lordship Lane and walk 10 metres and cross the level crossing. Turn left and walk 60 metres and turn right into Redvers Road. Walk 60 metres to the junction with Wellesley Road where this scene was filmed looking down Redvers Road.

By bus the most direct route is from Stop J on Tenison Way directly outside Waterloo Station aboard the No. 243 (to Wood Green Station). Disembark at Stop E (Redvers Road). Cross Lordship Lane, turn right and walk 20 metres before turning left into Redvers Road. Walk 60 metres to the junction with Wellesley Road where this scene was filmed looking down Redvers Road.

Then

Now

The motorbike and sidecar approaches travelling towards the camera.

Location 40: Policeman Spots Smoke

Series Four, Episode Five: *Christmas Duty*

Selwyn Road, Brent, London, NW10 8QY.

Later in the Series Four episode, *Christmas Duty*, a policeman is seen walking along a street (18 minutes 17 seconds into the episode) when he sees smoke pouring out of a rear window and he enters the backyard. This scene was filmed on the opposite side of the road to No. 28 Selwyn Road and the long red-bricked wall, trees lining the street and black fence in which he enters the backyard are still there to this day as is the lamp post, but now it is of a more modern design.

How to get there: The most direct route to this location is via bus from London Euston Station from Stop H aboard the No. 18 bus (to Sudbury). Disembark at Stop V (Knatchbull Road) on Craven Park Road and walk north 100 metres, turn right onto Craven Park and then after 10 metres turn left onto Bruce Road and walk for 180 metres before turning right onto Hazeldean Road. Finally, after 200 metres take a slight left turn onto Selwyn Road and after 30 metres you will find on your left the black fence which we see the policeman about to enter through.

Then

Now

The policeman walks towards the camera surveying smoke billowing from the Butler house's kitchen.

Location 41: Trainee Driver Instructions

Series Four, Episode Six: *The L Bus*

Berkshire Gardens, Palmers Green, London, NW13 6AA.

In the sixth episode of Series Four, called *The L Bus*, a bus containing Stan, Jack and four trainees travels down a suburban street and pulls into a kerb (3 minutes 56 seconds into the episode). The bus stops outside No. 81 Berkshire Gardens and this is just before the turn into St Cuthbert's Road. The houses at this location all match those in the episode and trees still line the road. However, for some reason, when Stan is seen getting out of the bus and giving the trainee driver his instructions, this was filmed at another location as we see a patch of grass by the pavement side and this is not present when we see the bus pulling to a halt.

How to get there: The most direct route to this location is via tube from King's Cross/St Pancras Station on the Piccadilly Line heading northbound to Wood Green. Exit Wood Green Tube Station and cross at the level crossing and walk 50 metres to Stop H (Wood Green Station) on High Road. Board the No. 141 bus (to Palmers Green), disembarking at Stop BS (Berkshire Gardens). Turn left and walk 35 metres along Green Lanes and turn left into Berkshire Gardens. Walk 250 metres to No. 81 where the bus stops in the episode.

By bus the most direct route is from Stop E outside King's Cross Station aboard either the No. 73 bus (to Stoke Newington) or No. 476 bus (to Northumberland Park) disembarking at Stop NK (Newington Green) and from this stop board the No. 141 bus (to Palmers Green). Disembark at Stop BS (Berkshire Gardens). Turn left and walk 35 metres along Green Lanes and turn left into Berkshire Gardens. Walk 250 metres to No. 81 where the bus stops in the episode.

Then

Now

The bus pulls into the kerb roughly where the black hatchback is parked on the right.

Location 42: The Second-Hand Bed Scene

Series Four, Episode Six: *The L Bus*

Albert Vittoria House, Pellatt Grove, Wood Green, London, N22 5PG.

Later, in *The L Bus*, we see Stan, Jack and the four trainees taking a bed base, headboard and mattress from flats and rushing up a path and placing the items on the trainee bus (14 minutes 38 seconds into the episode). This scene was filmed at Albert Vittoria House in Wood Green and those flats remain virtually unchanged to this day, including the small, black, wrought iron fence that runs around the perimeters of the residential garden area.

How to get there: The most direct route to this location is via tube from King's Cross/St Pancras Station on the Piccadilly Line heading northbound to Wood Green. Exit Wood Green Tube Station, turn right onto High Road and walk for 290 metres before turning right into Ewart Grove. Walk for 50 metres then turn right into Stuart Crescent and walk for 75 metres before turning left into Pellatt Grove. After a 215 metres walk you will find Albert Vittoria House on your right.

By bus the most direct route is from Stop G on York Way (the street that runs directly north on the eastside of King's Cross Station) aboard the No. 259 bus (to Edmonton Green). Disembark at Stop R (Finsbury Park Station) and from this stop board the No. 29 bus (to Wood Green) disembarking at Wood Green Station. Turn left and walk 470 metres along High Road then turn right into Stuart Crescent and walk for 75 metres before turning left into Pellatt Grove. After a 215 metres walk you will find Albert Vittoria House on your right.

Then

Now

**The second-hand bed is picked up here with the
trainees exiting the blue door and running up the path
to place the various parts onto the parked bus.**

Location 43: The Bus Suffers an Oil Leak

Series Four, Episode Six: *The L Bus*

Wolves Lane, Palmers Green, London, N22 5JD.

Finally, in *The L Bus*, the bus travels down a curved street lined by houses (15 minutes 37 seconds into the episode) before coming to a stop. The trainee driver notices a warning light on and when Stan and Jack get out to find out what the problem is they realise the engine has suffered an oil leak. The bus stops outside No. 39 Wolves Lane in Palmers Green. If you look closely you can see the Wolves Lane street sign in this scene and you can see the junction into Norfolk Avenue in the background and it was on the corner of this street where I believe they filmed Stan giving his trainee driver instructions earlier in this episode (roughly outside 1A Norfolk Avenue).

How to get there: The most direct route to this location is via tube from King's Cross/St Pancras Station on the Piccadilly Line heading northbound to Wood Green. Exit Wood Green Tube Station, cross at the level crossing and walk 50 metres to Stop H (Wood Green Station) on High Road. Board the No. 141 bus (to Palmers Green) disembarking at Stop BS (Berkshire Gardens). Turn left and walk 35 metres along Green Lanes and turn left into Berkshire Gardens and walk for 520 metres before turning right onto Wolves Lane. Directly opposite stands No. 39 Wolves Lane where this scene was filmed.

By bus the most direct route is from Stop E outside King's Cross Station aboard either the No. 73 bus (to Stoke Newington) or No. 476 bus (to Northumberland Park) disembarking at Stop NK (Newington Green) and from this stop board the No. 141 bus (to Palmers Green). Disembark at Stop BS (Berkshire Gardens). Turn left and walk 35 metres along Green Lanes and turn left into Berkshire Gardens and walk for 520 metres before turning right onto Wolves Lane. Directly opposite stands No. 39 Wolves Lane where this scene was filmed.

Then

Now

**The bus travels towards the camera rounding the curve
in the road before grinding to a halt by the kerb in the
front right of this photograph.**

Then

Now

**The view seen when Stan chats with the trainee driver –
note the house in the foreground has had an extension
added to it but the garden wall pillars remain in place.**

Location 44: The Kids' Outing Begins

Series Four, Episode Seven: *The Kids' Outing*

Perth Road, Wood Green, London, N22 5PY.

In the seventh episode of Series Four, called *The Kids' Outing*, a bus with Stan, Jack, the Butler family and a group of rowdy children aboard speeds along a street with balloons and streamers hanging from the windows (11 minutes 6 seconds into the episode). In this scene the bus passes the junction to Berwick Road travelling along Perth Road passing No. 45 and the camera follows the bus until it passes the junction to Solway Road. The clues to this location are the park seen on the right-hand side and at the end of the scene, in the distance, The Lordship public house (still present there today) can be seen on Lordship Lane.

How to get there: The most direct route to this location is via tube from King's Cross/St Pancras Station on the Piccadilly Line heading northbound to Wood Green. Exit Wood Green Tube Station and turn left onto Lordship Lane and walk 700 metres until reaching the junction with Perth Road. Turn left onto Perth Road and walk 130 metres to the location on the right (across the road from No. 45 Perth Road).

By bus the most direct route is from Stop J on Tenison Way directly outside Waterloo Station aboard the No. 243 (to Wood Green Station). Disembark at Stop NS (Perth Road) on Lordship Lane. Cross the road and walk east for 50 metres and turn left onto Perth Road and walk 130 metres to the location on the right (across the road from No. 45 Perth Road).

Then

Now

Stan's bus with smoke pouring from the exhaust is seen travelling down this road.

Location 45: The Exhaust Pipe Falls Off

Series Four, Episode Seven: *The Kids' Outing*

Berwick Road, Wood Green, London, N22 5QB.

The Kids' Outing continues and we see the bus travelling down a street (11 minutes 10 seconds into the episode) with smoke pouring from its rear and as the bus passes the camera the exhaust pipe falls off and skids along the road before coming to a halt. This location can be pinpointed as Berwick Road in Wood Green with the distinctive red-leafed tree (outside No. 21) still present today but increased in size obviously and further south of the tree you get a brief glimpse of a garden wall with a neat white brickwork frame around it which is still present today as well. From this wall it can be judged that the exhaust pipe came to a halt in the middle of the road almost directly outside No. 9 Berwick Road.

How to get there: The most direct route to this location is via tube from King's Cross/St Pancras Station on the Piccadilly Line heading northbound to Wood Green. Exit Wood Green Tube Station and turn left onto Lordship Lane and walk 700 metres until reaching the junction with Perth Road. Turn left onto Perth Road and walk 133 metres before turning left into Berwick Road and walk 60 metres to No. 9 Berwick Road to where the exhaust pipe skidded to a halt.

By bus the most direct route is from Stop J on Tenison Way directly outside Waterloo Station aboard the No. 243 (to Wood Green Station). Disembark at Stop NS (Perth Road) on Lordship Lane. Cross the road and walk east for 50 metres, then turn left onto Perth Road and walk 133 metres before turning left into Berwick Road. Walk 60 metres to No. 9 Berwick Road to where the exhaust pipe skidded to a halt.

Then

Now

A moment before the exhaust falls off the bus travels down Berwick Road.

Location 46: Bus Stops and Kids Misbehave

Series Four, Episode Seven: *The Kids' Outing*

Inverness Terrace, Wood Green, London, N22 5BT.

Finally, in *The Kids' Outing*, the bus turns a corner as the children aboard sing and smoke pours from the back of the bus (11 minutes 17 seconds into the episode) before it pulls to the side of the road and stops. As Stan and Jack get out and inspect the engine (11 minutes 24 seconds into the episode) they struggle to control the children. This scene was filmed outside No. 1 Inverness Terrace (which is part of Stirling Road) and it can be identified by the distinctive houses on the corner of Stirling Road in the background, the lamp post beside which the bus stops and behind Stan and Jack as they talk is a black garage door which today has been replaced and is white and is the garage for No. 1 Inverness Terrace.

How to get there: The most direct route to this location is via tube from King's Cross/St Pancras on the Piccadilly Line heading northbound to Wood Green. Exit Wood Green Tube Station and turn left onto Lordship Lane and walk 700 metres until reaching the junction with Perth Road. Turn left onto Perth Road and walk 133 metres before turning left into Berwick Road and walk 150 metres. Turn right into Stirling Road and walk 25 metres to No. 1 Inverness Terrace on your right.

By bus the most direct route is from Stop J on Tenison Way directly outside Waterloo Station aboard the No. 243 (to Wood Green Station). Disembark at Stop NS (Perth Road) on Lordship Lane. Cross the road and walk east for 50 metres and turn left onto Perth Road and walk 133 metres before turning left into Berwick Road and walk 150 metres. Turn right into Stirling Road and walk 25 metres to No. 1 Inverness Terrace on your right.

Then

Now

**The bus turns a corner at the far end of this street
and comes to a stop just after passing the lamp post
in the foreground of the photograph.**

Then

Now

**The black wrought iron gate remains outside No. 1
Inverness Terrace.**

Location 47: A Busman's Wedding

Series Five, Episode Three: *The Best Man*

St Mary's Church, Village Road, Denham, UB9 5BH.

It's a busman's wedding in the third episode of Series Five, *The Best Man*. The wedding party come out of an old church (21 minutes 40 seconds into the episode) which has a blue-faced clock on its tower with gold-plated clock hands and numbers in roman numerals. The wedding party walk down a path through the church to a decorated bus which waits outside. As the bus pulls away and the closing credits roll we see a row of cottages which the bus passes that are still there to this day and on the right of this row of houses now stand a blue plaque placed there by The Heritage Foundation declaring that the late, great, distinguished actor Sir John Mills lived there. The church is St Mary's in the village of Denham and was about six miles to the west of LWT's studios in Wembley. The church remains unchanged to the present day.

How to get there: The most direct route to this location is via train from London Marylebone Station aboard a Chiltern Railways service to Denham. Exit Denham Station, turn left and walk 120 metres, then turn right into Station Parade. From Stop A (Denham Station) board the No. 581 bus (to Friends Walk) and disembark at the undesignated stop for the Denham War Memorial. Turn right and walk 32 metres along Village Road to St Mary's Church.

Then

Now

The wedding party exit this archaic door of St Mary's Church.

Then

Now

The bus departs the church passing this row of houses which remain unchanged.

Location 48: The Dressmaker's Dummy at a Bus Stop

Series Five, Episode Six: *The Busmen's Ball*

Vivian Avenue, Wembley, London, HA9 6RH.

The sixth episode of Series Five, *The Busmen's Ball*, sees Mum and Olive standing in a queue at a bus stop with a dressmaker's dummy (14 minutes 15 seconds into the episode). This scene was filmed directly outside No. 109 Vivian Avenue and this can be identified by the red-bricked house in the background seen in the beginning of the scene, the ramp on the pavement leading into the driveway at No. 109 next to a grass verge on which the bus stop is located and a tree next to Olive and Mum – all are present at this location today.

How to get there: The most direct route to this location is via train from London Euston Station aboard a London Overground service to Stonebridge Park Station. Exit Stonebridge Park Station turning right on Argenta Way, after 40 metres turn left onto North Circular Road and then after 100 metres turn left onto Harrow Road. Cross Harrow Road and walk for 500 metres and then turn right onto Victoria Avenue. Walk for 270 metres and turn left into Vivian Avenue and a further walk of 42 metres will bring you to outside No. 109 where this scene was filmed.

By bus the most direct route is from Stop H at London Euston Station aboard the No. 18 bus (to Sudbury). Disembark at the undesignated stop for Flamsted Avenue and cross Harrow Road, turn right and walk for 125 metres before turning right onto Victoria Avenue. Walk for 125 metres and turn left into Vivian Avenue and a further walk of 42 metres will bring you to outside No. 109 where this scene was filmed.

Then

Now

Olive and Mum wait at a bus stop to the left of the tree with their dressmaker's dummy.

Location 49: Blakey Finds the Dressmaker's Dummy

Series Five, Episode Six: *The Busmen's Ball*

Vivian Avenue, Wembley, London, HA9 6RQ.

In the following scene in *The Busmen's Ball*, we see a bus approaching Blakey (14 minutes 43 seconds into the episode) who waits at a bus stop in a tree-lined street also flanked by distinctive houses. This scene was also filmed on Vivian Avenue with Blakey standing directly outside No. 45 and this can be worked out by careful scrutiny of the number of grass verges along the roadside and hedge in the garden at No. 45 along with the garage that can be seen at the rear of the property when Blakey looks to board the bus (15 minutes 2 seconds into the episode) which is still present today.

How to get there: The most direct route to this location is via train from London Euston Station aboard a London Overground service to Stonebridge Park Station. Exit Stonebridge Park Station turning right on Argenta Way, after 40 metres turn left onto North Circular Road and then after 100 metres turn left onto Harrow Road. Cross Harrow Road and walk for 500 metres and then turn right onto Victoria Avenue. Walk for 270 metres and turn left into Vivian Avenue and a further walk of 300 metres will bring you to outside No. 45 where this scene was filmed.

By bus the most direct route is from Stop H at London Euston Station aboard the No. 18 bus (to Sudbury). Disembark at the undesignated stop for Flamsted Avenue and cross Harrow Road, turn left and walk for 45 metres before turning right onto St Michael's Avenue. Walk for 110 metres and turn left into Vivian Avenue and a further walk of 60 metres will bring you to outside No. 45 where this scene was filmed.

Then

Now

Blakey stands on the path beyond the tree in the foreground beside a temporary bus stop.

Then

Now

The garages seen behind Blakey as he looks to board the bus remain to this day.

Location 50: Time for a Skive

Series Five, Episode Thirteen: *Vacancy for Inspector*

Princedale Road, Notting Hill, London, W11 4NH.

Stan and Jack's bus travels down a narrow built-up street (1 minute 31 seconds into the thirteenth episode of Series Five called *Vacancy for Inspector*) before coming to a halt. This street is Princedale Road and the camera picks up the bus as it passes No. 108 Princedale Road heading in the direction of Holland Park Avenue. The area today has not changed too much at all with all the three-storey housing still present but a side road that existed in the direction the bus has just travelled from has been closed off and is no longer a through road.

How to get there: The most direct route to this location is via tube from Liverpool Street Station on the Central Line heading westbound to Holland Park. Exit Holland Park Station, turn right along Holland Park Avenue and walk for 185 metres. Turn right into Princedale Road and walk for 400 metres to No. 108 where the bus passes in the episode.

By bus the most direct route is from Stop L outside London Marylebone Station aboard the No. 2 bus (to West Norwood). Disembark at Marble Arch Station (Stop W) and from this stop board either the No. 94 (to Acton Green) or the No. 148 (to Shepherd's Bush) and disembark at Stop HC (Norland Square). Turn left and walk 55 metres back in the direction you have just travelled, cross Holland Park Avenue and turn left into Norland Square. Walk for 165 metres and turn right into Queensdale Road and after walking for 134 metres turn left into Princedale Road. Walk for 255 metres to No. 108 where the bus passes in the episode.

Then

Now

Another difference is that antique lamp posts have replaced the regulation lamp posts present in 1971.

Location 51: Hiding Around the Corner

Series Five, Episode Thirteen: *Vacancy for Inspector*

Junction of Princedale Road/Penzance Place, Notting Hill, London, W11 4NS.

Jack leads Stan to the corner of a road in *Vacancy for Inspector* as he explains to Stan (2 minutes 30 seconds into the episode) that the bus queue is around the corner and if they wait where they are they can allow another bus to pick up those passengers first and is seen later in the episode with Stan and Christine at the location. This scene was filmed on the junction of Princedale Road and Penzance Place and this can be identified by the curved inward wall on the side of the house on the corner. Although it has Stan and Jack looking around the corner into Penzance Place, the bus stop with passengers waiting was actually positioned further down Princedale Road directly outside No. 78. Clever camera work can have you believe anything.

How to get there: The most direct route to this location is via tube from Liverpool Street Station on the Central Line heading westbound to Holland Park. Exit Holland Park Station, turn right along Holland Park Avenue and walk for 185 metres. Turn right into Princedale Road and walk for 280 metres to the junction of Princedale Road and Penzance Place to the curved wall on the corner where Jack and Stan peer around the corner.

By bus the most direct route is from Stop L outside London Marylebone Station aboard the No. 2 bus (to West Norwood). Disembark at Marble Arch Station (Stop W) and from this stop board either the No. 94 (to Acton Green) or the No. 148 (to Shepherd's Bush) and disembark at Stop HB (Holland Park). Turn right and walk 30 metres and cross Holland Park Avenue, turning right into Princedale Road. Walk for 280 metres to the junction of Princedale Road and Penzance Place to the curved wall on the corner where Jack and Stan peer around the corner.

Then

Now

**Stan's bus is parked to the left and Jack and Stan edge
around this wall in the episode.**

Then

Now

The passengers queue at a bus stop where the black-framed shop window can be seen and is directly down the same road where Stan's bus parks.

Location 52: Jack and Blakey Sneaking Across the Road

Series Five, Episode Thirteen: *Vacancy for Inspector*

Junction of Pottery Lane/Penzance Place, Notting Hill, London, W11 4PE.

Finally, in *Vacancy for Inspector*, a bus pulls up on the junction of a narrow street and Inspector Blake and Jack get out (14 minutes 12 seconds into the episode). The bus stops on the junction of Pottery Lane by the rear of No. 11 Penzance Place and they sneak across Penzance Place and edge their way along against the wall to catch Stan who is skiving around the corner with Christine in Princedale Road. The area remains unchanged although the façade of the houses look quite different.

How to get there: The most direct route to this location is via tube from Liverpool Street Station on the Central Line heading westbound to Holland Park. Exit Holland Park Station, turn right along Holland Park Avenue and walk for 185 metres. Turn right into Princedale Road, walk for 280 metres to the junction of Princedale Road and Penzance Place and turn right. Walk ten metres to the junction of Pottery Lane where the bus stopped in this scene.

By bus the most direct route is from Stop L outside London Marylebone Station aboard the No. 2 bus (to West Norwood). Disembark at Marble Arch Station (Stop W) and from this stop board either the No. 94 (to Acton Green) or the No. 148 (to Shepherd's Bush) and disembark at Stop HB (Holland Park). Turn right and walk 30 metres and cross Holland Park Avenue, turning right into Princedale Road. Walk for 280 metres to the junction of Princedale Road and Penzance Place and turn right. Walk ten metres to the junction of Pottery Lane where the bus stopped in this scene.

Then

Now

Blakey and Jack sneak across this road to catch Stan in the act.

Location 53: Smoking Bus

Series Six, Episode One: *No Smoke Without Fire*

Tilehouse Lane, Denham, Buckinghamshire, UB9 5DU.

The first episode of Series Six, *No Smoke Without Fire*, sees Stan and Jack with two trainee clippies aboard a bus with an engine that is smoking badly and gets parked on a leafy lane (15 minutes 52 seconds into the episode). Trees line both sides of the road and the bus is seen coming to a stop as it passes a green public footpath sign on a green pole next to the roadside. This scene was filmed just north of the village of Denham and today, where the bus stopped, is now akin to a gravel-covered lay-by, whereas in the episode the area is soil covered in fallen leaves. The public footpath sign is still present by the roadside but the pole it is attached to is now grey in colour and the road now has white road markings unlike in the episode.

How to get there: The most direct route to this location is via train from London Marylebone Station aboard a Chiltern Railways service to Denham. Exit Denham Station, turn left, then walk 120 metres and turn right into Station Parade. From Stop A (Denham Station) board the No. 331 bus (to Uxbridge) and disembark at Stop N (Tilehouse Lane) and from this stop board the No. 581 (to Denham Station). Disembark at the undesignated stop (Wyatts Covert), turn right and walk 275 metres along Tilehouse Lane until reaching, on your left, the public footpath sign seen in the episode where the smoking bus parks.

Then

Now

Stan's smoking bus pulls in here stopping with the rear of the bus where the puddle is in this photograph taken late in 2015.

Then

Now

The two clippies stand side-by-side directly across the road from the parked bus just to the left of the two slender tree trunks with one waving at Stan and Jack.

Location 54: Blakey Spots a Piano Aboard a Bus

Series Six, Episode Three: *Private Hire*

Ridge Road, Crouch End, London, N8 9LE.

In the third episode of Series Six, *Private Hire*, Inspector Blake stands at a bus stop and sees a bus pass him by with a piano sticking out of the door (12 minutes 37 seconds into the episode). The bus has just turned out of a road lined by red-bricked houses with ornate markings and turret-like structures above the windows. This scene was filmed on Ridge Road around ten metres west of No. 1 Ridge Road with the bus having turned right out of Ferme Park Road. Today the location has changed very little although the trees seen to the right of the inspector behind a garden fence have been removed as has the fence which has been replaced by a brick wall.

How to get there: The most direct route to this location is via train from London King's Cross Station aboard a Great Northern service to Harringay Station. Exit Harringay Station using the Quernmore Road exit and walk for 270 metres along Quernmore Road. Turn right into Oakfield Road and walk for 165 metres before turning left into Ridge Road. Walk for 320 metres along Ridge Road before turning right to cross the road where a lamp post stands just west of No. 1 Ridge Road where the inspector stood looking west.

By bus the most direct route is from Stop G on York Way (the street that runs directly north on the eastside of King's Cross Station) aboard the No. 259 bus (to Edmonton Green) disembarking at Stop X (Fonthill Road). Turn right and walk 10 metres along Seven Sisters Road and turn left into Fonthill Road. Walk 150 metres and cross here, then turn right into Wells Terrace, walking 80 metres to Finsbury Park Bus Station. From Stop B board the W3 bus (to Northumberland Park) disembarking at Stop F (Mount View Road/Ferme Park Road). Turn right and cross here before turning left and walking 20 metres before turning right into Ridge Road. Walk 10 metres and cross here to the lamp post where the inspector stood looking west.

Then

Now

The inspector stands here and watches a bus pass by carrying a piano.

Location 55: Moving a Piano

Series Six, Episode Three: *Private Hire*

Nelson Road, Crouch End, London, N8 9RX.

Seconds later, in *Private Hire*, Stan and Jack use their bus as a removal van and they prepare to move a piano from their bus (12 minutes 56 seconds into the episode) and into a house. With a chair used to stop the piano rolling down the pavement, which is on a steep decline, this precarious scene was filmed outside No. 1 Nelson Road. The cream coloured garden wall present in the scene still remains at the property today, and in the background the row of houses in the adjacent street (Ridge Road), with their lavish arched window frames protruding above roof level, are still present and much unchanged aside from the loss of the red brickwork.

How to get there: The most direct route to this location is via train from London King's Cross Station aboard a Great Northern service to Harringay Station. Exit Harringay Station using the Quernmore Road exit and walk for 270 metres along Quernmore Road. Turn right into Oakfield Road and walk for 165 metres before turning left into Ridge Road. Walk for 270 metres and turn right into Nelson Road and after walking 115 metres (on your left) is No. 1 where this location was filmed.

By bus the most direct route is from Stop G on York Way (the street that runs directly north on the eastside of King's Cross Station) aboard the No. 17 bus (to Archway) disembarking at Stop U (Archway Station). From this stop board the No. 41 bus (to Tottenham Town Hall) and disembark at Stop S (Tottenham Lane YMCA). Turn right and cross Tottenham Lane, walk for 50 metres and turn right into Ferme Park Road. Walk for 257 metres, turn left into Weston Park and walk for 85 metres, then turn right into Nelson Road. Walk for 275 metres and on your right is No. 1 where this location was filmed.

Then

Now

Jack and Stan use a chair to stop a piano they are moving from rolling away at this location.

Location 56: Carried Away by a Piano

Series Six, Episode Three: *Private Hire*

Nelson Road, Crouch End, London, N8 9RX.

Seconds later in *Private Hire*, Blakey arrives on the scene to confront Stan and Jack and whisks a chair away that is propped up against a piano. Suddenly, the piano starts rolling down the pavement towards him and he leaps on it and it gathers speed (13 minutes 43 seconds) before it crashes into the side of the bus that he has just arrived on directly outside No. 5 Nelson Road. Aside from that property's façade changing from grey to white painted brickwork, everything remains much the same to this day.

How to get there: The most direct route to this location is via train from London King's Cross Station aboard a Great Northern service to Harringay Station. Exit Harringay Station using the Quernmore Road exit and walk for 270 metres along Quernmore Road. Turn right into Oakfield Road and walk for 165 metres before turning left into Ridge Road. Walk for 270 metres and turn right into Nelson Road and after walking 125 metres (on your left) is No. 5 where the piano impacts the side of the bus.

By bus the most direct route is from Stop G on York Way (the street that runs directly north on the eastside of King's Cross Station) aboard the No. 17 bus (to Archway) disembarking at Stop U (Archway Station). From this stop board the No. 41 bus (to Tottenham Town Hall) and disembark at Stop S (Tottenham Lane YMCA). Turn right and cross Tottenham Lane, walk for 50 metres and turn right into Ferme Park Road. Walk for 257 metres, turn left into Weston Park and walk for 85 metres then turn right into Nelson Road. Walk for 265 metres and on your right is No. 5 where the piano impacts the side of the bus.

Then

Now

The piano rolls downhill with Blakey clinging to it.

Location 57: S F and T Morris Bookmakers

Series Six, Episode Three: *Private Hire*

Barretts Green Road, Brent Park, London, NW10 7AE.

Stan and Jack park their bus outside a bookmakers shop in *Private Hire* (13 minutes 56 seconds into the episode) and enter inside. The bookmakers is at the end of a long line of old houses on Barretts Green Road but this location has changed beyond recognition. The housing and bookmakers have been demolished and replaced by an industrial estate, and roughly where the bookmakers stood there is now a single-storey café called Riviera Café. Directly across the road in the episode from where the bus parks a cash and carry can be seen and this building is still present today with the black iron staircase outside leading to office space on the second floor seen in the episode, still there today. Incidentally, this bookmaker shop location was also used in an episode of another LWT hit sitcom – *Please Sir*.

How to get there: The most direct route to this location is via train from London Euston Station aboard a London Overground service to Harlesden. Exit Harlesden Station and turn right into Acton Lane. Walk for 365 metres, turn right into Barretts Green Road and walk for 35 metres where, on your right, is the Riviera Café where S F and T Morris Bookmakers shop once stood.

By bus the most direct route is from Stop P outside London Marylebone Station aboard the No. 18 bus (to Sudbury) disembarking at Stop H (Willesden Junction Station/Furness Road). Turn right and walk 85 metres before turning left into Tubbs Road. Walk for 260 metres, turn left into Station Road and after a 40-metre walk turn left into Station Approach. Walk for 75 metres to Stop N (Willesden Junction) and board the No. 487 bus (to South Harrow). Disembark at Stop PA (Waxlow Road), turn right and walk 120 metres along Acton Lane before turning right into Barretts Green Road and walk for 35 metres where, on your right, is the Riviera Café where S F and T Morris Bookmakers shop once stood.

Then

Now

**The row of houses seen on the right amidst which stood
the bookmakers were demolished at least two decades
ago and replaced with an industrial estate**

Location 58: Blakey Drives Stan's Bus Away

Series Six, Episode Three: *Private Hire*

Barretts Green Road, Brent Park, London, NW10 7AE.

Finally, in *Private Hire*, we see Blakey out to teach Stan and Jack a lesson. They have parked their bus outside a bookmakers, and whilst they back another loser Blakey arrives on the scene and gets into the cab of Stan's bus and drives it back to the depot (15 minutes 1 second into the episode). The bus drives off along Barretts Green Road passing a brown-bricked windowless building which remains today but has been painted white. In the distance, Acton Lane can be seen although the most prominent structure seen in the background on the far side of Acton Lane has been demolished and the area redeveloped with a similar-sized structure.

How to get there: The most direct route to this location is via train from London Euston Station aboard a London Overground service to Harlesden. Exit Harlesden Station and turn right into Acton Lane. Walk for 365 metres, turn right into Barretts Green Road and walk for 35 metres where, on your right, is the Riviera Café directly where the camera pans around to film Stan's bus being driven off towards Acton Lane.

By bus the most direct route is from Stop P outside London Marylebone Station aboard the No. 18 bus (to Sudbury) disembarking at Stop H (Willesden Junction Station/Furness Road). Turn right and walk 85 metres before turning left into Tubbs Road. Walk for 260 metres, turn left into Station Road and after a 40-metre walk turn left into Station Approach. Walk for 75 metres to Stop N (Willesden Junction) and board the No. 487 bus (to South Harrow). Disembark at Stop PA (Waxlow Road), turn right and walk 120 metres along Acton Lane before turning right into Barretts Green Road and walk for 35 metres where, on your right, is the Riviera Café directly where the camera pans around to film Stan's bus being driven off towards Acton Lane.

Then

Now

**The building on the right can be seen as Blakey drives
Stan's bus away.**

Chapter Two – South of the Thames

Location 59: The South Bank Television Centre

Series Seven

Upper Ground, Lambeth, London, SE1 9LT.

London Weekend Television was to move from their Wembley Studios into a new custom-built facility late in 1972. The company had taken out a 100-year lease on the new studio buildings in 1968 which were owned by Coal Pension Properties and for LWT it would remain their home as a broadcasting franchise until late in 2002. The studios would also produce many television series for many different production companies.

The studios were to be where Series Seven of *On the Buses* was filmed but it presented the production crews with a problem. There is no doubting the studios were state-of-the-art and superbly equipped but, unlike their previous facility at Wembley, the studios had no access for the double decker Lodekka buses to enter for the internal depot shots due to size restrictions on the double doors from the road into the studios. They came up with an innovative solution to this by driving single decker buses into the studios and from a hoist above lowering a mock upper deck made of plywood onto it to make the single deck bus appear to be a double decker.

Of course, the South Bank Television Centre would churn out many other classic LWT sitcoms such as *Billy Liar*, *Mind Your Language*, *A Fine Romance*, *Metal Mickey*, *The Two of Us* and other comedy series including *The Stanley Baxter Picture Show*, *Candid Camera*, *Cannon and Ball* and *It'll Be Alright on the Night* among others. The studios also produced much-loved dramas such as *Upstairs Downstairs*, *Within These Walls*, *Bouquet of Barbed Wire* and *Dick Turpin*. Also there was a myriad of arts and light entertainment series such as *World of Sport*, *You Bet*, *Saint and Greavsie*, *Supersonic*, *The South Bank Show*, *Surprise Surprise*, *Game for a Laugh*, *The Russell Harty Show*, *Play Your Cards Right*, *Blind Date* and *Gladiators*.

It was late in 2002 when LWT ceased to exist as a broadcasting company as the whole franchise system was disbanded and LWT, along with the rest of the regional networks, became known as ITV1. LWT continued to produce its local news and sports programmes at the studios, which had been renamed The London Television Centre in 1992, but the studios had also begun producing programmes for many different production companies including the BBC. Productions to emerge from the newly-branded studios include *Whose Line Is It Anyway?*, *Have I got News For You*, *Strictly Come Dancing: It Takes Two*, *Father Ted*, *Parkinson*, *Daybreak*, *Catchphrase*, *Tipping Point*, *The Jonathan Ross Show*, *The Chase* and *The Paul O'Grady Show* to name but a few.

Late in 2012, rumours were to surface that, 44 years into their 100-year lease, ITV was seeking to leave The London Television Centre and that the site owners had put the site up for sale. It was rumoured that ITV were looking at moving to another site, possibly even sharing the newly-formed BT Sport's studios at Olympic Park but nothing materialised on that front and for the time being at least, The London Television Centre, formerly The South Bank Television Centre, remains home to ITV.

How to get there: The most direct route to this location is by foot from Waterloo Station. Exit Waterloo Station and onto Waterloo Road, turning left, and walk for 50 metres. Turn right into Sandell Street and walk 60 metres before turning left into Cornwall Road. Walk for 250 metres, then turn left into Upper Ground and walk 60 metres to The London Television Centre on your left.

Now

**The former LWT custom-built South Bank Studios, now
The London Television Centre.**

Location 60: The County Court

Series Seven, Episode One: *Olive's Divorce*

Knatchbull Road, Camberwell, London, SE5 9QY.

In the first episode of Series Seven, called *Olive's Divorce*, a bus with Stan, Olive and Mum aboard is seen pulling up outside a county court building (10 minutes 18 seconds into the episode). This scene was filmed at 50 Knatchbull Road at a building called Longfield Hall and it made for a convincing court. Today, the building is masked somewhat by trees but, that aside, the listed building and those that surround it in the street remain largely unchanged. The clues to finally finding this episode were the park at the end of the road, whilst the hall itself is such a distinctive shape it was unmistakable once found. This location proved a real headache to find as it was never actually a courthouse and is now used as a multi-purpose venue, which threw me somewhat off the scent.

How to get there: The most direct route to this location is via train from London St Pancras Station (Lower Level) aboard a Thameslink service to Loughborough Junction. Exit Loughborough Junction Station, turn right onto Coldharbour Lane and walk for 90 metres. Turn right into Loughborough Road, cross at the level crossing then turn right and walk 40 metres to Stop C boarding the P5 bus (to Elephant and Castle). Disembark at Stop SW9 (Lilford Road) and turn right, walking for 53 metres. Turn right into Lilford Road, walking for 140 metres before turning left into Knatchbull Road and after a 90-metre walk you will see Longfield Hall on your left which doubled as the county court Olive was divorced in.

By bus the most direct route is from Stop R outside Elephant and Castle Station aboard the P5 bus (to Patmore Estate/Drury House). Disembark at Lilford Road (undesignated stop) and turn left to walk 70 metres along Loughborough Road. Turn right into Lilford Road and walk for 140 metres before turning left into Knatchbull Road. After a 90-metre walk you will see Longfield Hall on your left which doubled as the county court Olive was divorced in.

Then

Now

The court where Olive finally divorces Arthur.

Then

Now

Stan and Mum lead a sobbing and reluctant Olive from the bus up this pavement.

Location 61: Blakey Escorts Olive Home

Series Seven, Episode One: *Olive's Divorce*

Carden Road, Peckham, London, SE15 3UB.

Later in *Olive's Divorce*, Blakey escorts Olive home, walking along a dark street. In the background is a brick wall with the rear of a house on the other side of the wall. The house has an outhouse structure attached with a small window on the side of it and as Blakey turns to lead Olive back down the road they have just walked up, they pass a tree that is growing towards the outside of the pavement (23 minutes 25 seconds into the episode) and houses on the opposite side of Nunhead Lane can also be seen. This scene was filmed in Carden Road in Peckham, with the property they pass in the background being the rear of No. 36 Nunhead Lane which runs adjacent to Carden Road. The wall seen in the episode has been raised in height by around 60 centimetres but, that apart, the location remains much the same.

How to get there: The most direct route to this location is via train from London St Pancras Station (Lower Level) aboard a Thameslink service to Nunhead Station. Exit Nunhead Station and from Stop NA board the P12 bus (to Surrey Quays) and disembark at Stop EP (Carden Road). Turn left and walk 10 metres along Nunhead Lane before turning right into Carden Road and walk 15 metres to the filming location by the brick wall.

By bus the most direct route is from Stop L on Bishopsgate outside Liverpool Street Station. Board the No. 78 bus (to St Mary's Road) and disembark at Stop ES (Carden Road). Turn right, walk 30 metres along Nunhead Lane before crossing the road and turn right into Carden Road and walk 15 metres to the filming location by the brick wall.

Then

Now

Blakey leads Olive down this road in darkness, passing the tree which still remains.

Location 62: Sandra's House

Series Seven, Episode One: *Olive's Divorce*

Carden Road, Peckham, London, SE15 3UD.

Once more, in *Olive's Divorce*, Blakey takes Olive around to a clippie called Sandra's house where she is entertaining Stan. As the inspector walks up the path (23 minutes 36 seconds into the episode) we can see the house has enough clues to pinpoint the location, even though the scene was filmed on a dark evening. The front door has a distinctive arch over it, the front windows have a row of small stained glass panels at the top (unique to houses in this street which was a great help) and a pair of wooden gates at the side of the house leading up a side alleyway to the rear of the property. This all helps to identify this location as No. 18 Carden Road, which was no more than 50 metres away from the previous location on the opposite side of the same street. This street was to be used again later in Series Seven.

How to get there: The most direct route to this location is via train from London St Pancras Station (Lower Level) aboard a Thameslink service to Nunhead Station. Exit Nunhead Station and from Stop NA board the P12 bus (to Surrey Quays) and disembark at Stop EP (Carden Road). Turn left and walk 10 metres along Nunhead Lane before turning right into Carden Road, cross the road and walk 60 metres to the filming location on your left – No. 18 Carden Road.

By bus the most direct route is from Stop L on Bishopsgate outside Liverpool Street Station. Board the No. 78 bus (to St Mary's Road) and disembark at Stop ES (Carden Road). Turn right, walk 30 metres along Nunhead Lane before crossing the road and turn right into Carden Road, cross the road and walk 60 metres to the filming location on your left – No. 18 Carden Road.

Then

Now

Note the unique stained glass panel windows and the same front door still in place.

Location 63: The Closing Credits of Series Seven Start

Series Seven, Episode One: *Olive's Divorce*

Oldfields Road, Sutton, London, SM1 2NU.

The closing credits begin to roll in Series Seven with a bus travelling along a dual carriageway road. Houses can be seen lining the left of the road and just before cutting to another location the bus passes an industrial looking building. This scene was filmed in Sutton on Oldfields Road and today the location remains largely unchanged aside from the industrial building which was home to the Pobjoy Mint. That building today has either been demolished and totally rebuilt as a storage facility or underwent extensive refurbishment.

How to get there: The most direct route to this location is via tube from King's Cross/St Pancras Station on the Northern Line heading southbound to Morden. Exit Morden Station and turn left to walk 10 metres to the level crossing. Turn right and cross here before turning left and walking 10 metres to Stop H. Board the No. 80 bus (to Downview and Highdown Prisons) and disembark at Stop SC (Stayton Road). Turn right and walk 60 metres along Oldfields Road. Cross Strayton Road and walk a further 40 metres until just having passed the storage facility building on your left. The bus was filmed travelling west to east on this stretch of road ahead.

By bus the most direct route is from Stop D on Waterloo Road directly outside Waterloo Station aboard the No. 59 bus (to Streatham Hill/Telford Avenue). Disembark at Stop W (Streatham Hill/Telford Avenue) and from this stop board the No. 201 bus (to Morden). Disembark at Stop H (London Road/Morden Station) and from this stop board the No. 80 bus (to Downview and Highdown Prisons) and disembark at Stop SC (Stayton Road). Turn right and walk 60 metres along Oldfields Road. Cross Strayton Road and walk a further 40 metres until just having passed the storage facility building on your left. The bus was filmed travelling west to east on this stretch of road ahead.

Then

Now

Where the McDonald's sign stands in 1973 stood a petrol station sign.

Then

Now

**The storage facility where Pobjoy Mint stood and the
stretch of houses remain unchanged.**

Location 64: The Closing Credits of Series Seven End

Series Seven, Episode One: *Olive's Divorce*

London Road, Morden, London, SM4 5BH.

As the closing credits roll throughout Series Seven a bus can be seen passing a row of shops on the left with a park approaching ahead. The bus can clearly be seen passing an F W Woolworth's store and this is now occupied by an all-in-one convenience store called Timmy's, which is on London Road in Morden. The park seen ahead is Morden Hall Park and the roundabout also seen in the closing credits remains to the current day, but has been reduced a great deal in size.

How to get there: The most direct route to this location is via tube from King's Cross/St Pancras Station on the Northern Line heading southbound to Morden. Exit Morden Station, turn left and walk 110 metres to Timmy's store on your left (formerly Woolworth's seen in the closing credits).

By bus the most direct route is from Stop D on Waterloo Road directly outside Waterloo Station aboard the No. 59 bus (to Streatham Hill/Telford Avenue). Disembark at Stop Q (Brixton Station) and from this stop board the No. 118 bus (to Morden) disembarking at Stop N (Morden Station). Turn right and walk 130 metres to Timmy's store on your left (formerly Woolworth's seen in the closing credits).

Then

Now

A Luxton and District bus passes down this street in the closing credits sequence.

Location 65: Olive Quoting the Rule Book

Series Seven, Episode Two: *The Perfect Clippie*

Reigate Avenue, Sutton, London, SM1 3JL.

The second episode of Series Seven, *The Perfect Clippie*, sees a bus travelling down a dual carriageway as Olive is heard quoting the rulebook to Jack (15 minutes 9 seconds into the episode). In the background is a sloping grassy bank with periodic sets of steps leading up to a row of houses and a white three-storey block of flats at the end of these houses. This brief location shot was filmed on Reigate Avenue heading westwards about 200 metres past the Rose Hill Roundabout which remains there today. The only change to this location is a row of trees that now mask the houses on the other side of the sloped grassy bank.

How to get there: The most direct route to this location is via train from London St Pancras Station (Lower Level) aboard a Thameslink service to St Helier Station. Exit St Helier Station, turn right, walk 15 metres and cross the zebra crossing. Turn right and walk 15 metres to Stop MN. Board the No. 154 bus (to West Croydon) and disembark at Stop RP (Rose Hill/Rose Hill Roundabout), turning right and walk up Rose Hill for 35 metres before crossing the level crossing. Follow the path directly ahead, walking for 85 metres until reaching Reigate Avenue. Turn right and walk up Reigate Avenue for 60 metres and you will be roughly at the point where the camera would have been positioned to film the bus travelling down Reigate Avenue.

By bus the most direct route is from Stop T on Concert Hall Approach across the road from Waterloo Station aboard the No. 77 bus (to Tooting Station). Disembark at Stop M (Tooting Broadway Station), turn right and walk 130 metres along Garratt Lane and onto Mitcham Road to Stop E (Mitcham Road/Tooting Broadway). Board the No. 280 bus (to Belmont) and disembark at Stop RP (Rose Hill/Rose Hill Roundabout), turning right and walk up Rose Hill for 35 metres before crossing at the level crossing. Follow the path directly ahead, walking for 85 metres until reaching Reigate Avenue. Turn right and walk up Reigate Avenue for 60 metres and you will be roughly at the point where the camera would have been positioned to film the bus travelling down Reigate Avenue.

Then

Now

Stan's bus is seen travelling down this road as Olive pesters Jack.

Location 66: Jack About to Complain to Stan

Series Seven, Episode Two: *The Perfect Clippie*

St John's Church, Waterloo Road, London, SE1 8TY.

When Olive quotes the rulebook to Jack about smoking upstairs on the bus he rushes downstairs to complain to Stan and opens the door to the bus (15 minutes 55 seconds into the episode) as it continues on its journey in *The Perfect Clippie*. As the doors open the bus passes a large church with stone pillars. This church is St John's in Waterloo, directly across the Waterloo Road from Waterloo Station. The street layout has changed greatly since the episode was filmed here with the pavement being widened greatly and trees planted to the left of the church. The church itself, of course, is unchanged.

How to get there: The most direct route to this location is on foot from Waterloo Station. Exit Waterloo Station at the Station Approach exit, turn left and walk 50 metres before turning right to cross the zebra crossing. Walk 20 metres through the underpass onto Waterloo Road, turn right and walk 20 metres to the level crossing. Cross at the level crossing and turn right. After a 15-metre walk the church seen in the episode stands on your left.

Then

Now

The church which Stan's bus speeds past as Jack opens the door to complain to him.

Location 67: Jack Hangs out of the Bus Door

Series Seven, Episode Two: *The Perfect Clippie*

Kennington Road, Kennington, London, SE11 6SF.

A direct continuation from the previous location in *The Perfect Clippie* sees Jack hang out of the door (15 minutes 56 seconds into the episode) and orders Stan to get Olive off of his back. As he does so the bus can be seen passing a park in the background followed by a public house and a row of single-level shops before continuing along to pass a distinctive row of houses set back from the road with large front gardens and hedges. The road is also lined by trees. The public house seen is now called the Grand Union, which stands on Kennington Road and the park seen is the Geraldine Harmsworth Park. The bus travels southwards down Kennington Road until around No. 133 Kennington Road when it cuts to Olive ticking Jack off again inside the bus. It is clear though that Stan's dialogue in this scene was evidently filmed at a different location as the scenery on the other side of the road when the camera is on Stan is not that of Kennington Road.

How to get there: The most direct route to this location is via tube from Waterloo Station on the Bakerloo Line heading southbound to Lambeth North. Exit Lambeth North Station and turn left on Westminster Bridge Road, walking for 5 metres to the level crossing. Cross here and walk 5 metres before turning left onto Kennington Road. Walk for 367 metres and on your left (on the corner of Brook Drive) you will find the Grand Union public house seen briefly in the episode.

By bus the most direct route is from Stop D on Waterloo Road directly outside Waterloo Station aboard the No. 59 (to Streatham Hill/Telford Avenue). Disembark at Stop S (Kennington Road/Imperial War Museum) and the stretches of houses ahead were seen in the background in the episode. Turn left and walk 75 metres and on your right (on the corner of Brook Drive) you will find the Grand Union public house seen briefly in the episode.

Then

Now

As Jack hangs out of the front door this public house is seen in the background.

Location 68: Olive Quotes More Rules at a Roundabout

Series Seven, Episode Two: *The Perfect Clippie*

Rose Hill, Sutton, London, SM5 1AD.

Olive continues to quote the rulebook to Jack as the bus navigates around a roundabout (17 minutes 22 seconds into the episode) and turns into Reigate Avenue. In the background a public house sits on a corner of a road and that and the roundabout were the clues to finding this location. This brief scene was filmed at The Rose Hill Roundabout in Sutton and the public house has been demolished and a superstore now stands on that site. The roundabout remains but it has morphed from being completely circular to a stretched rounded shape. The internal shots as Olive goes to ring the bell to stop the bus were filmed elsewhere though – probably in the Kennington area.

How to get there: The most direct route to this location is via train from London St Pancras Station (Lower Level) aboard a Thameslink service to St Helier Station. Exit St Helier Station, turn right, walk 15 metres and cross the zebra crossing. Turn right and walk 15 metres to Stop MN. Board the No. 154 bus (to West Croydon) and disembark at Stop RP (Rose Hill/Rose Hill Roundabout), turning left and walk up Rose Hill for 65 metres before turning left again to cross at the level crossing. Walk for 15 metres, turning left into Reigate Avenue to arrive roughly at a point where the camera would have been when filming the bus travelling around the roundabout and turning into Reigate Avenue.

By bus the most direct route is from Stop T on Concert Hall Approach across the road from Waterloo Station aboard the No. 77 bus (to Tooting Station). Disembark at Stop M (Tooting Broadway Station), turn right and walk 130 metres along Garratt Lane and onto Mitcham Road to Stop E (Mitcham Road/Tooting Broadway). Board the No. 280 bus (to Belmont) and disembark at Stop RP (Rose Hill/Rose Hill Roundabout), turning right and walk up Rose Hill for 65 metres before turning left again to cross at the level crossing. Walk for 15 metres, turning left into Reigate Avenue to arrive roughly at a point where the camera would have been filming the bus travelling around the roundabout and turning into Reigate Avenue.

Then

Now

The Rose public house seen in the background has long since replaced by a Co-op superstore.

Location 69: The Disgruntled Scot

Series Seven, Episode Two: *The Perfect Clippie*

Renfrew Road, Kennington, London, SE11 4NA.

Finally, in *The Perfect Clippie*, Olive takes it upon herself to ring the bell for the bus to stop and Stan is forced to break suddenly. A well-built Scotsman aboard the bus is unsettled by the sudden stop (17 minutes 33 seconds into the episode) and outside the bus can be seen a row of houses with an unusual configuration of front doors set back beside garage doors for the same properties. This scene was filmed in Renfrew Road and logic presumes that the bus stopped on the opposite side of the road from the houses past the entrance into Kempsford Road, with No. 33 Renfrew Road across the road from where the angry Scot sits on the bus.

How to get there: The most direct route to this location is via tube from Waterloo Station on the Northern Line heading southbound to Kennington Station. Exit Kennington Station, turning right and after five metres cross Kennington Park Road via the level crossing. Turn right, walking 75 metres before turning left onto Othello Close, then walk for 180 metres before turning right into Kennington Lane. Walk for 80 metres, cross the road and turn left into Renfrew Road. After a walk of 130 metres, just past the junction of Kempsford Road, is where the bus stopped in the episode.

By bus the most direct route is from Stop P directly outside Elephant and Castle Station aboard the No. 196 bus (to Norwood Junction Station). Disembark at Stop BH (Renfrew Road), turn left and walk 60 metres along Kennington Lane and cross the road. Turn left into Renfrew Road and after a walk of 130 metres, just past the junction of Kempsford Road, is where the bus stopped in the episode.

Then

Now

The distinctive houses seen out of the bus window in the background during this scene.

Location 70: Olive and Mum at the Roadside

Series Seven, Episode Four: *The Poster*

Gilbert Road, Kennington, London, SE11 4NQ.

In the fourth episode of Series Seven, *The Poster*, Olive and Mum stand at the roadside watching Stan's promotional poster being pasted onto a board beside them. In the background (23 minutes 35 seconds into the episode) a bus with Stan, Blakey and Jack aboard approaches down a narrow and curving road. This is Gilbert Road in Kennington but it has changed so much today. The right- and left-hand sides of the road have seen new houses built, trees that lined the right of the road as the camera looked at it have been reduced in number, a small brick wall remains only in small segments and new houses stand on the corner of Gilbert Road leading into Renfrew Road. Olive and Mum stand on the pavement outside roughly where No. 43 Gilbert Road stands now.

How to get there: The most direct route to this location is via tube from Waterloo Station on the Northern Line heading southbound to Kennington Station. Exit Kennington Station, turning right and after five metres cross Kennington Park Road via the level crossing. Turn right, walking 75 metres before turning left onto Othello Close and walking for 180 metres before turning right into Kennington Lane. Walk for 80 metres, cross the road and turn left into Renfrew Road and after a walk of 230 metres cross Gilbert Road where No. 43 is directly ahead, this being where Mum and Olive stood. From here look to your right in the direction the bus travels from.

By bus the most direct route is from Stop P directly outside Elephant and Castle Station aboard the No. 196 bus (to Norwood Junction Station). Disembark at Stop BH (Renfrew Road), turn left and walk 60 metres along Kennington Lane and cross the road. Turn left into Renfrew Road and after a walk of 230 metres cross Gilbert Road where No. 43 is directly ahead, this being where Mum and Olive stood. From here look to your right in the direction the bus travels from.

Then

Now

Where Olive and Mum stood as Stan's bus approaches.

Location 71: Stan's Bus Crash

Series Seven, Episode Four: *The Poster*

Renfrew Road, Kennington, London, SE11 4NA.

A few seconds later in the episode, *The Poster*, Stan drives his bus along a narrow road and when he sees a promotional poster containing his face being pasted up at the roadside he is distracted and crashes his bus into a small garden in front of a row of houses (23 minutes 50 seconds into the episode). The bus was seen travelling along, passing Mum and Olive at the roadside standing at the end of Gilbert Road before crashing into the garden of No. 19 Renfrew Road. Today these properties along Renfrew Road have no such gardens so I am fairly confident the garden seen in the episode was created especially for this scene and also acted as a buffer, stopping the bus doing any damage to the property. To confirm this watch very closely frame-by-frame and as the bus skids on the lawn you can see the turf strips move and the concrete pavement can be seen beneath.

How to get there: The most direct route to this location is via tube from Waterloo Station on the Northern Line heading southbound to Kennington Station. Exit Kennington Station, turning right and after five metres cross Kennington Park Road via the level crossing. Turn right, walking 75 metres before turning left onto Othello Close and walking for 180 metres before turning right into Kennington Lane. Walk for 80 metres, cross the road and turn left into Renfrew Road and after a walk of 225 metres cross Renfrew Road and No. 19 is directly ahead where Stan's bus crashes into the mock garden.

By bus the most direct route is from Stop P directly outside Elephant and Castle Station aboard the No. 196 bus (to Norwood Junction Station). Disembark at Stop BH (Renfrew Road), turn left and walk 60 metres along Kennington Lane and cross the road. Turn left into Renfrew Road and after a walk of 225 metres cross Renfrew Road and No. 19 is directly ahead where Stan's bus crashes into the mock garden.

Then

Now

Stan's bus crashes into a garden here which was created purely for this scene.

Location 72: The Football Match

Series Seven, Episode Five: *The Football Match*

Edgar Kail Way, East Dulwich, London, SE22 8BD.

The fifth episode of Series Seven, *The Football Match*, centres around a less than sporting contest between The Luxton Lions and Basildon Bashers. The two teams exit the dressing rooms onto the pitch (exactly 19 minutes into the episode) and the scene takes up virtually the remainder of the episode. This location was extremely difficult to track down but the clues were the five storey flats in the background that run along one of the touchlines whilst on the other touchline is what looks like the rear of a small football stadium's grandstand. At the far end of the pitch were more small blocks of flats on an inclining road. These clues finally helped pinpoint the location. The football pitch played on was presumably a training pitch for Dulwich Hamlet FC with the rear of their main stand visible in various shots on the right touchline. The five-storey flats visible on the left touchline remain today though are now masked by trees and are Leconsfield House, Holderness House and Birdsall House. The flats at the far end of the pitch running along the far side of Dog Kennel Hill also remain today. Sadly, the pitch and changing rooms have long since disappeared to be replaced by a Sainsbury's superstore, Starbucks coffee shop and car park.

How to get there: The most direct route to this location is via train from London Bridge Station aboard a Southern Trains service to East Dulwich Station. Exit East Dulwich Station, turn left and walk 85 metres along Grove Vale. Turn left into Edgar Kail Way and walk for 120 metres and on your left you will see Dulwich Hamlet FC stadium, the rear of which you see in the episode, and on your right is a car park with Sainbury's store where the football pitch would have stood.

By bus the most direct route is from Stop T directly outside London Fenchurch Street Station aboard the No. 40 bus (to Dulwich Library). Disembark at Stop L (Quorn Road), turn left and walk 30 metres before turning left to cross at the level crossing. Turn left into Edgar Kail Way and walk for 120 metres and on your left you will see Dulwich Hamlet FC stadium, the rear of which you see in the episode, and on your right is a car park with Sainsbury's store where the football pitch would have stood.

Then

Now

The dressing rooms once stood here which is now an overgrown piece of land at the rear of Sainsbury's superstore.

Then

Now

The car on the left in the foreground is parked roughly where Stan prepares to kick-off on the centre spot of the football pitch.

Then

Now

Jack stood roughly just to the left of the small tree in the foreground where the goalline was, as he allowed the Basildon Bashers to score another goal.

Location 73: Olive at the Manager's House

Series Seven, Episode Six: *On the Omnibuses*

East Mascalls Lane, Lindfield, Haywards Heath, West Sussex, RH16 2QN.

The sixth episode of Series Seven, *On the Omnibuses*, sees Stan dream of life working as a bus driver in the 1920s and he is shocked to see Olive chained to the manager's house in a quiet country lane staging a protest (exactly 22 minutes into the episode). The house is a distinctively-shaped cottage with a wall and creeping vines running alongside its garden with an elaborate pattern on the side of the cottage. It remains to this day in Mascalls Lane near Haywards Heath. Although extensions have been added to the property it remains instantly recognisable although a tree has been removed from just in front of the wall and the iron fence atop the wall is no longer there (if it ever was).

How to get there: The most direct route to this location is via train from London St Pancras Station (Lower Level) aboard a Southern Trains service to Haywards Heath Station. Exit Haywards Heath Station and turn left to walk 20 metres before crossing at the level crossing, then turning left onto Market Place. Walk 90 metres to the bus stop directly outside Sainbury's and board the No. 31 bus (to Hurst Green). Disembark at the Request Stop (on Scamps Hill) and turn right to walk 40 metres. Turn left onto East Mascalls Lane and walk 1050 metres and on your right is East Mascalls Cottage seen in the episode.

Then

Now

The manager's house where Olive staged her protest.

Location 74: Blakey's Bike in Tow

Series Seven, Episode Six: *On the Omnibuses*

Sloop Lane, Haywards Heath, West Sussex, RH17 7NP.

On the Omnibuses sees Blakey manage to catch up with Stan's bus on his bicycle and his bike is seen attached to the rear of the bus being towed past a country public house (23 minutes 14 seconds into the episode). This fleeting scene was filmed with the bus passing what is now The Sloop Inn on Sloop Lane, around four miles to the east of the West Sussex town of Haywards Heath. Today it would seem there have been cosmetic changes to the public house as what appeared to be a connecting village shop with its own doorway in the episode, now appears that the doorway has been removed and the shop has been incorporated into an extension of the public house. Aside from that the location is identical.

How to get there: The most direct route to this location is via train from London St Pancras Station (Lower Level) aboard a Southern Trains service to Haywards Heath Station. Exit Haywards Heath Station and turn left to walk 20 metres before crossing at the level crossing, turning left onto Market Place. Walk 90 metres to the bus stop directly outside Sainbury's and board the No. 31 bus (to Hurst Green). Disembark at the Request Stop on Lewes Road in the village of Scaynes Hill (opposite the Doctor's PH) and turn right to walk 75 metres. Turn left onto Church Lane, walk 1250 metres and turn left into Sloop Lane. Walk for a further 400 metres and on your left is the Sloop Inn which the omnibus passes in this episode.

Then

Now

The Sloop Inn remains in business in 2016.

Location 75: Blakey Encounters a Low-Level Bridge

Series Seven, Episode Six: *On the Omnibuses*

Sloop Lane, Haywards Heath, West Sussex, RH17 7NP.

Later in *On the Omnibuses* we see Stan drive an open-topped bus along a country lane towards a low-level railway bridge (23 minutes 25 seconds into the episode), sending passengers scurrying downstairs for cover. Inspector Blake is not so lucky and is left clinging from the bridge as the bus leaves him behind. This scene was filmed on Sloop Lane and the bridge remains today with trains from the privately-funded Bluebell Railway still crossing it with the only real difference being the trees lining the road increasing in number and size.

How to get there: The most direct route to this location is via train from London St Pancras Station (Lower Level) aboard a Southern Trains service to Haywards Heath Station. Exit Haywards Heath Station and turn left to walk 20 metres before crossing at the level crossing, turning left onto Market Place. Walk 90 metres to the bus stop directly outside Sainbury's and board the No. 31 bus (to Hurst Green). Disembark at the Request Stop on Lewes Road in the village of Scaynes Hill (opposite the Doctor's PH) and turn right to walk 75 metres. Turn left onto Church Lane, walk 1250 metres and turn left into Sloop Lane. Walk for a further 880 metres and on ahead is the railway bridge which Blakey hangs from on its south side.

Then

Now

Blakey hung from this bridge and in 2015 here is a Bluebell Railway service crossing the bridge.

Location 76: Blakey Climbs to Safety

Series Seven, Episode Six: *On the Omnibuses*

Sloop Lane, Haywards Heath, West Sussex, RH17 7NP.

Seconds after clinging from a bridge in *On the Omnibuses*, Blakey is seen climbing over the edge of a railway bridge to safety as a train approaches (24 minutes 2 seconds into the episode). In the distance another railway bridge can be seen in the distance with open fields on either side of the rail track. The scene was filmed on the bridge that straddles Sloop Lane with a single track still in use today by the Bluebell Railway services but a row of bushes and hedges run alongside the track into the distance today, unlike 1973, though the bridge in the distance remains.

How to get there: The most direct route to this location is via train from London St Pancras Station (Lower Level) aboard a Southern Trains service to Haywards Heath Station. Exit Haywards Heath Station and turn left to walk 20 metres before crossing at the level crossing, turning left onto Market Place. Walk 90 metres to the bus stop directly outside Sainbury's and board the No. 31 bus (to Hurst Green). Disembark at the Request Stop on Lewes Road in the village of Scaynes Hill (opposite the Doctor's PH) and turn right to walk 75 metres. Turn left onto Church Lane, walk 1250 metres and turn left into Sloop Lane. Walk for a further 890 metres until passing under the railway bridge which Blakey hangs from and turn left up a steep bank, but it is not advised for you to attempt to photograph this location as it means trespassing on the railway line belonging to the Bluebell Railway and is highly dangerous.

Then

Now

The bridge seen in *On the Omnibuses*.

Location 77: Stan Leaves Luxton

Series Seven, Episode Seven: *Goodbye Stan*

Nunhead Lane, Peckham, London, SE15 3TU.

It is the seventh episode of Series Seven, aptly called *Goodbye Stan*, when everyone's favourite bus driver leaves the Luxton depot for the last time. As a passenger heading to the train station, the bus he is aboard pulls out of the depot into a narrow side street and turns onto the main road (26 minutes 41 seconds into the episode). This scene was filmed at the long since demolished Nunhead Bus Garage on Nunhead Lane in South Peckham. The only thing that remains on the site of the old depot (demolished in the late 1990s) is the clock tower and a plaque on the wall next to No. 28 Nunhead Lane. The bus exits Banfield Road having pulled out of the rear exit of the depot and passes a four-storey block of flats called Lancefield House which still stands on the exit of Banfield Road to the present day as can be seen in the photograph.

How to get there: The most direct route to this location is via train from London St Pancras Station (Lower Level) aboard a Thameslink service to Nunhead Station. Exit Nunhead Station and from Stop NA board the P12 bus (to Surrey Quays) and disembark at Stop EP (Carden Road). Turn right and walk 5 metres along Nunhead Lane and on your left is the clock tower and plaque. Straight ahead is the exit of Banfield Road where the bus exits in the episode and beyond that Lancefield House which is also seen.

By bus the most direct route is from Stop L on Bishopsgate outside Liverpool Street Station. Board the No. 78 bus (to St Mary's Road) and disembark at Stop ES (Carden Road). Cross Nunhead Lane, turn left and walk 20 metres and on your right is the clock tower and plaque. Look to your far right and you will see the exit of Banfield Road where the bus exits in the episode and beyond that Lancefield House which is also seen.

Then

Now

As the bus pulls out of the depot we see a glimpse of these metal doors in Banfield Road.

Then

Now

The bus pulls out of this street with Stan aboard as he leaves the depot for the last time.

Location 78: Turning the Water Mains Off

Series Seven, Episode Eight: *Hot Water*

Carden Road, Peckham, London, SE15 3UD.

Inspector Blake and Jack venture out of Jack's house to switch off the water at the mains in the street (17 minutes 44 seconds into the eighth episode of Series Seven, *Hot Water*). The property they exit is No. 12 Carden Road and is identifiable by the garden wall which remains the same today though now painted white. Also, the wall running adjacent between No 10. and No. 12 along the garden path is still the same with its ornate design and we get a brief glimpse of the number ten on the door next to the house Blakey and Jack exit. The water mains panel in the street that they raise has changed in design and the lamp post has gone now but the tree seen in the background in the street remains to this day. This location is seen again later in the episode when a policeman interrupts them and later still when water ends up springing up six or seven feet in the air watched by a crowd of people.

How to get there: The most direct route to this location is via train from London St Pancras Station (Lower Level) aboard a Thameslink service to Nunhead Station. Exit Nunhead Station and from Stop NA board the P12 bus (to Surrey Quays) and disembark at Stop EP (Carden Road). Turn left and walk 10 metres along Nunhead Lane before turning right into Carden Road, cross the road and walk 45 metres to the filming location on your left – No. 12 Carden Road.

By bus the most direct route is from Stop L on Bishopsgate outside Liverpool Street Station. Board the No. 78 bus (to St Mary's Road) and disembark at Stop ES (Carden Road). Turn right, walk 30 metres along Nunhead Lane and cross the road, turning right into Carden Road, cross the road and walk 45 metres to the filming location on your left – No. 12 Carden Road.

Then

Now

Blakey exits the white door which today has been brought forward on the property.

Then

Now

**The view down the street where the policeman walks
up later in the scene.**

Location 79: A Walk to Public Toilets

Series Seven, Episode Eleven: *The Allowance*

Peckham Rye Park, Peckham, London, SE15 3UA.

Jack and his driver Sid leave their bus and walk through a park to public toilets (3 minutes 21 seconds into the eleventh episode of Series Seven, *The Allowance*). There is a wide scattering of trees with houses visible on the horizon and they walk past a five-foot high black wrought iron fence. This scene was filmed in Peckham Rye Park close to the public toilets which still remain to this day. Jack and Sid would have walked along the edge of Straker's Road which runs into the park and down directly outside those public toilets they were walking towards. This area of the park has changed a little with a car park replacing a number of trees and through road, whilst new paths have been added to this area of the park.

How to get there: The most direct route to this location is via train from London St Pancras Station (Lower Level) aboard a Thameslink service to Nunhead Station. Exit Nunhead Station and from Stop NA board the P12 bus (to Surrey Quays) and disembark at Stop WK (Peckham Rye/East Dulwich Road). Turn left and walk 50 metres along Peckham Rye. Cross at the level crossing and carry on walking along Peckham Rye for 260 metres, then cross at the zebra crossing. Straight ahead is a path that leads into Peckham Rye Common, walk along this path for around 50 metres and take a turn right. After 50 metres you should see the black wrought iron fence in front of the public toilets where this scene was shot.

By bus the most direct route is from Stop S outside London St Pancras Station aboard the No. 63 bus (to Forest Hill Tavern). Disembark at the Request Stop (on Friern Road), turn left and walk 30 metres and turn right to walk along a path that crosses Peckham Rye Park. Walk for 45 metres until a junction in the path where you take the left turn and follow the path for 50 metres where you will find the public toilets on your right with the black wrought iron fence. The padlocked gate is that which Jack and Sid enter through.

Then

Now

**Jack and Sid discuss Jessie as they walk to the toilets
with the tree seen in the background still present today.**

Then

Now

And the path they walk down to the toilets on the left.

Location 80: Olive and Jessie Exit Public Toilets

Series Seven, Episode Eleven: *The Allowance*

Peckham Rye Park, Peckham, London, SE15 3UA.

The next scene shot we see in *The Allowance* is when Jessie and Olive emerge from public toilets in a leafy park (3 minutes 59 seconds into the episode) discussing having to pay to use the toilets. The toilet exit was a confined space with a leafy bush encroaching onto a path and they are located no more than 5 metres from the previous location in Peckham Rye Park. The toilets remain in operation to this day but with one entrance for both sexes and, although the pebble-dashed exterior has gone, the structure of the building remains but the ladies entrance is no longer in use and an extension has been added to that area which is used as the park wardens' offices.

How to get there: The most direct route to this location is via train from London St Pancras Station (Lower Level) aboard a Thameslink service to Nunhead Station. Exit Nunhead Station and from Stop NA board the P12 bus (to Surrey Quays) and disembark at Stop WK (Peckham Rye/East Dulwich Road). Turn left and walk 50 metres along Peckham Rye. Cross at the level crossing and carry on walking along Peckham Rye for 260 metres, then cross at the zebra crossing. Straight ahead is a path that leads into Peckham Rye Common. Walk along this path for around 50 metres and take a turn right and after 50 metres you should see the black wrought iron fence in front of the public toilets and the ladies entrance is on the left side of the building.

By bus the most direct route is from Stop S outside London St Pancras Station aboard the No. 63 bus (to Forest Hill Tavern). Disembark at the Request Stop (Friern Road), turn left and walk 30 metres and turn right to walk along a path that crosses Peckham Rye Park. Walk for 45 metres until a junction in the path where you take the left turn and follow the path for 50 metres. On your right is a black wrought iron fence in front of the public toilets and the ladies entrance is on the left side of the building.

Then

Now

Jessie and Olive exit the toilets with the bush still evident in 2015.

Location 81: Jessie's Complaint

Series Seven, Episode Eleven: *The Allowance*

Peckham Rye Park, Peckham, London, SE15 3UA.

When Olive and Jessie bump into Jack and Sid outside the public toilets (4 minutes 50 seconds into *The Allowance*) it sees Jessie complain about having to pay to use the toilets. This scene was shot by the right-hand gate into the area where the public toilets are found. They slowly walk alongside the black wrought iron fence heading eastwards and stop to discuss Jessie putting in a complaint to Blakey at the left-hand gate. This area remains largely unchanged today aside from the road on which the buses are parked in rear of shot which remains but is now downscaled to a public walkway.

How to get there: The most direct route to this location is via train from London St Pancras Station (Lower Level) aboard a Thameslink service to Nunhead Station. Exit Nunhead Station and from Stop NA board the P12 bus (to Surrey Quays) and disembark at Stop WK (Peckham Rye/East Dulwich Road). Turn left and walk 50 metres along Peckham Rye. Cross at the level crossing and carry on walking along Peckham Rye for 260 metres, then cross at the zebra crossing. Straight ahead is a path that leads into Peckham Rye Common. Walk along this path for around 50 metres and take a turn right and after 50 metres you should see the black wrought iron fence in front of the public toilets and the right-hand gate is where the beginning of this scene was filmed.

By bus the most direct route is from Stop S on Midland Road outside London St Pancras Station aboard the No. 63 bus (to Forest Hill Tavern). Disembark at the Request Stop (Friern Road), turn left and walk 30 metres, then turn right to walk along a path that crosses Peckham Rye Park. Walk for 45 metres until a junction in the path where you take the left turn and follow the path for 50 metres. On your right is a black wrought iron fence in front of the public toilets and the right-hand gate is where the beginning of this scene was filmed.

Then

Now

The gate to the ladies toilet is locked today and the lamp post seen behind Jack remains in place but is of a newer design.

Location 82: A Bus on its Way to Toilets

Series Seven, Episode Eleven: *The Allowance*

Morden Hall Road, Morden, London, SM4 5HX.

Later, in *The Allowance*, a bus, with a roundabout in the foreground and a park in the background, travels along a road (15 minutes 52 seconds into the episode). This very brief scene was filmed with the bus having just passed the roundabout on Morden Road at the junction of London Road as it heads down Morden Hall Road. The tall stone pillars at the entrance into Morden Hall Park and Morden Hall itself can be seen in the episode and today the only noticeable change is that the roundabout visible has decreased greatly in size since the episode was filmed here.

How to get there: The most direct route to this location is via tube from King's Cross/St Pancras Station on the Northern Line heading southbound to Morden. Exit Morden Station, turn left and walk 115 metres to the corner of Kenley Road. Looking to your right down Morden Hall Road is roughly where the camera filmed this brief scene.

By bus the most direct route is from Stop D on Waterloo Road directly outside Waterloo Station aboard the No. 59 bus (to Streatham Hill/Telford Avenue). Disembark at Stop Q (Brixton Station) and from this stop board the No. 118 bus (to Morden) disembarking at Stop N (Morden Station). Turn right and walk 135 metres to the corner of Kenley Road. Looking to your right down Morden Hall Road is roughly where the camera filmed this brief scene.

Then

Now

**Note the roundabout is smaller in size but now
somewhat elevated.**

Location 83: Sandra Visiting Public Toilets

Series Seven, Episode Eleven: *The Allowance*

Peckham Rye Park, East Dulwich Road, Peckham, London, SE15 3UA.

Sid's bus pulls up at public toilets in a park (15 minutes 54 seconds into *The Allowance*) and Sandra rushes into them as Blakey, who is in turn watched by a policeman, watches from behind a tree. This scene was filmed at the public toilets on East Dulwich Road which runs through Peckham Rye Park. The building, which was public toilets, still stands but have undergone renovations to convert it into a nursery. The tree which Blakey hides behind remains there with bushes now growing around its base immediately to the right of the toilets.

How to get there: The most direct route to this location is via train from London Bridge Station aboard a Southern Trains service to Peckham Rye Station. Exit Peckham Rye Station, turn right on Rye Lane and walk for 45 metres before crossing at the zebra crossing. Turn right and walk 35 metres to Stop V (Peckham Rye) and board either the No. 12 (to Dulwich Library), the No. 63 (to Honor Oak) or the No. 363 (to Crystal Palace). Disembark at Stop WN (Peckham Rye/East Dulwich Road) and turn right and walk 12 metres along Peckham Rye before turning left into East Dulwich Road. Walk 25 metres and the toilets seen in the episode are on your left.

By bus the most direct route is from Stop S on Midland Road outside London St Pancras Station aboard the No. 63 bus (to Forest Hill Tavern). Disembark at Stop WN (Peckham Rye/East Dulwich Road) and turn right and walk 12 metres along Peckham Rye before turning left into East Dulwich Road. Walk 25 metres and the toilets seen in the episode are on your left.

Then

Now

**The former toilets where Sid's bus pulls up – now
shrouded in bushes but still recognisable.**

Location 84: Blakey Takes to his Bike

Series Seven, Episode Eleven: *The Allowance*

East Dulwich Road, Peckham, London, SE15 3UA.

Finally, in *The Allowance*, after noting down Sandra's toilet visit from behind a tree, Blakey rushes to his bike and boards it, peddling off in the direction that the bus has just headed off in (16 minutes 51 seconds into the episode), followed by a policeman. The street is lined by trees and in the distance you can see the clock tower outside the old Nunhead Bus Garage in Nunhead Lane. This scene was shot on East Dulwich Road with Peckham Rye Park on either side of the road and today it remains identical aside from the growth of the trees by the roadside.

How to get there: The most direct route to this location is via train from London Bridge Station aboard a Southern Trains service to Peckham Rye Station. Exit Peckham Rye Station, turn right on Rye Lane and walk for 45 metres before crossing at the zebra crossing. Turn right and walk 35 metres to Stop V (Peckham Rye) and board either the No. 12 (to Dulwich Library), the No. 63 (to Honor Oak) or the No. 363 (to Crystal Palace). Disembark at Stop WN (Peckham Rye/East Dulwich Road) and turn right and walk 12 metres along Peckham Rye before turning left into East Dulwich Road. Walk 25 metres and the toilets seen in the episode are on your left. Looking east from this point is roughly where the camera was positioned to film Blakey peddling off on his bicycle.

By bus the most direct route is from Stop S on Midland Road outside London St Pancras Station aboard the No. 63 bus (to Forest Hill Tavern). Disembark at Stop WN (Peckham Rye/East Dulwich Road) and turn right and walk 12 metres along Peckham Rye before turning left into East Dulwich Road. Walk 25 metres and the toilets seen in the episode are on your left. Looking east from this point is roughly where the camera was positioned to film Blakey peddling off on his bicycle.

Then

Now

Blakey rides off pursued by a policeman on this stretch of road.

Location 85: A Trip along Lavender Hill

Series Seven, Episode Thirteen: *Gardening Time*

Lavender Hill, Battersea, London, SW11 5TE.

The thirteenth episode of Series Seven and last ever episode of *On the Buses*, called *Gardening Time*, sees a bus travel along a main street lined by shops and houses (11 minutes 22 seconds into the episode) with Jack aboard, looking to collect an array of plants. This scene was filmed with the bus travelling westwards along Lavender Hill in Battersea from it passing the entrance to Longbeach Road until stopping outside shops at No. 203 Lavender Hill. It appears that the camera was positioned outside the Battersea Arts Centre when filming this scene. The street has changed very little although a zebra crossing seen in the episode has been replaced by a level crossing.

How to get there: The most direct route to this location is via train from Waterloo Station aboard a South West Trains service to Clapham Junction Station. Exit Clapham Junction Station via the Shopstop Shopping Centre onto St John's Hill. Turn left, walk 330 metres and on your left is the Battersea Arts Centre. On the eastside of this building is where the camera was positioned to film this scene.

By bus the most direct route is from Stop T on Concert Hall Approach across the road from Waterloo Station aboard the No 77 bus (to Tooting Station). Disembark at Stop D (Battersea Arts Centre), turn right and walk 45 metres along Lavender Hill to the level crossing. Cross here and walk straight ahead to the eastside of the Battersea Arts Centre where the camera was positioned to film this scene.

Then

Now

In 2015 a red Transport for London bus stands where Jack's Luxton and District green-liveried bus travelled.

Location 86: Jack Steals Plants

Series Seven, Episode Thirteen: *Gardening Time*

The Battersea Arts Centre, Battersea, London, SW11 5TN.

Moments later in *Gardening Time*, Jack gets off his bus and crosses the road to a splendid looking building with pillars at its rounded frontage (11 minutes 38 seconds into the episode). He steals potted plants dotted around the front of the building before making his escape. This building is the Battersea Arts Centre on Lavender Hill but when this episode was filmed here it was the Battersea Town Hall, which it remained until 1979. The only structural difference to the Arts Centre being an added ramp access to the building for wheelchair users.

How to get there: The most direct route to this location is via train from Waterloo Station aboard a South West Trains service to Clapham Junction Station. Exit Clapham Junction Station via the Shopstop Shopping Centre onto St John's Hill. Turn left, walk 330 metres and on your left is the Battersea Arts Centre that is seen in the episode.

By bus the most direct route is from Stop T on Concert Hall Approach across the road from Waterloo Station aboard the No. 77 bus (to Tooting Station). Disembark at Stop D (Battersea Arts Centre), turn right and walk 50 metres along Lavender Hill to the level crossing. Cross here and to your left is the Battersea Arts Centre that is seen in the episode.

Then

Now

Jack prepares to steals plants from outside this building. Photographed in 2015 with scaffolding, as repairs continued after a serious fire in 2014 that gutted the lower floor.

Location 87: Blakey Shopping for Plants

Series Seven, Episode Thirteen: *Gardening Time*

Lavender Hill, Battersea, London, SW11 5TE.

Inspector Blake shops for plants and comes out of a florist lining up his potted plants on the pavement (12 minutes 4 seconds into *Gardening Time*). When Jack's bus comes along he is refused entry as the bus is already full with Jack's stolen flora. The florist shop was located at No. 171 Lavender Hill (on the corner of Longbeach Road) but today that property is The Lavender public house and, looking westwards, what was then the Battersea Town Hall is visible on the opposite side of the road. Aside from the paving slabs on the pavement being replaced by an unusual red-bricked covering, the location is much the same outside what was the florist shop.

How to get there: The most direct route to this location is via train from Waterloo Station aboard a South West Trains service to Clapham Junction Station. Exit Clapham Junction Station via the Shopstop Shopping Centre onto St John's Hill. Turn left, walk 332 metres and on your right is a level crossing. Cross here, turn left and walk 60 metres. On your right is The Lavender public house which is seen in this episode.

By bus the most direct route is from Stop T on Concert Hall Approach across the road from Waterloo Station aboard the No. 77 bus (to Tooting Station). Disembark at Stop D (Battersea Arts Centre), turn left and walk 10 metres along Lavender Hill. On your right is The Lavender public house which is seen in this episode.

Then

Now

**Note the wall remains to this day outside what was a
flower shop in 1973.**

Then

Now

Blakey lined up his potted plants at this point on the pavement.

Then

Now

Blakey flags down Jack's bus here.

Location 88: The Rag and Bone Man Arrives

Series Seven, Episode Thirteen: *Gardening Time*

Carden Road, Peckham, London, SE15 3UD.

Later in *Gardening Time* a rag and bone man leads his horse-drawn cart down a road (17 minutes 16 seconds into the episode). The camera picks up on him as he walks from the south end of Carden Road and he is roughly adjacent to No. 40 Carden Road in Peckham. Much remains the same today at this location with hedges still growing outside the garden in the background although the property in the rear of shot is now masked by trees growing there.

How to get there: The most direct route to this location is via train from London St Pancras Station (Lower Level) aboard a Thameslink service to Nunhead Station. Exit Nunhead Station and from Stop NA board the P12 bus (to Surrey Quays) and disembark at Stop EP (Carden Road). Turn left and walk 10 metres along Nunhead Lane before turning right into Carden Road and walk 135 metres (adjacent to No. 33 Carden Road). Looking across to No. 40 Carden Road is roughly the angle the camera had when filming this scene.

By bus the most direct route is from Stop L on Bishopsgate outside Liverpool Street Station. Board the No. 78 bus (to St Mary's Road) and disembark at Stop ES (Carden Road). Turn right, walk 30 metres along Nunhead Lane before crossing the road and turn right into Carden Road. Walk 135 metres (adjacent to No. 33 Carden Road). Looking across to No. 40 Carden Road is roughly the angle the camera had when filming this scene.

Then

Now

The rag and bone man walked down this street at this precise location.

Location 89: Arguing over Manure

Series Seven, Episode Thirteen: *Gardening Time*

Carden Road, Peckham, London, SE15 3UD.

Finally in *Gardening Time*, Blakey and Jack argue outside their houses over who is going to have the manure deposited on the street by the rag and bone man's horse. Jack emerges from No. 36 and Blakey from No. 34 Carden Road (17 minutes 43 seconds into the episode) but by the time they struggle to squeeze past each other the rag and bone man has removed the manure. Oddly enough, the rag and bone man is now heading in the opposite direction back up Carden Road from where he has just come. This location is identifiable as we see No 34 on the door of the Butler house which Blakey re-enters at the end of the scene.

How to get there: The most direct route to this location is via train from London St Pancras Station (Lower Level) aboard a Thameslink service to Nunhead Station. Exit Nunhead Station and from Stop NA board the P12 bus (to Surrey Quays) and disembark at Stop EP (Carden Road). Turn left and walk 10 metres along Nunhead Lane before turning right into Carden Road. Cross the road and walk 160 metres to the filming location on your left – Nos. 34 and 36 Carden Road.

By bus the most direct route is from Stop L on Bishopsgate outside Liverpool Street Station. Board the No. 78 bus (to St Mary's Road) and disembark at Stop ES (Carden Road). Turn right, walk 30 metres along Nunhead Lane before crossing the road. Turn right into Carden Road, cross the road and walk 160 metres to the filming location on your left – Nos. 34 and 36 Carden Road.

Then

Now

The two properties today amidst renovations in 2015.

Chapter Three – Borehamwood and Beyond

Location 90: Elstree Studios

The Three Spin-Off Films

Shenley Road, Borehamwood, Hertfordshire, WD6 1JG.

The history of Elstree Studios stretches back to 1925 when it was opened – financed by a British film producer called Herbert Wilcox and the Hollywood producer J D Williams. Since then the studios have scaled the heights and plunged to the depths of despair before rising from the ashes to flourish again.

Shortly after opening the studios, in the Hertfordshire town of Borehamwood on the outskirts of London, it ran into funding problems and it was a Scottish cinema owner called John Maxwell who took over the studios. He called them the British International Pictures and the studios' fortunes were to take a turn for the better. The site was greatly expanded in size in 1927 and it began to produce films with great stars of the big screen involved, such as Laurence Olivier, Charles Laughton, Stewart Granger and Ray Milland, whilst the later-to-be legendary director Alfred Hitchcock directed Britain's first 'talkie' film called *Blackmail*. The early 1930s were a boom period for the studios with hundreds of films being produced by the facility but a fire and a slump in the film industry meant a bad end to the 1930s. With the Second World War breaking out the studios were to be used for war purposes and sadly during this time the studio owner Maxwell passed away.

After the war the studios were taken over by Warner Brothers who had bought most of the late owner's shares from his widow and the big film company set about rebuilding and renovating the facility which was to become known as the Associated British Picture Corporation. Once more the studios were thriving with some of the world's greatest actors starring in studio productions, and classic films across the genres were produced. These included *Moby Dick*, *The Dam Busters*, *Ice Cold in Alex*, *Moonraker*, *Look Back in Anger*, *Summer Holiday* and *Sands of the Desert* and much more right through the 1950s and 60s. It was in the 1960s that the studios began to establish itself for its television productions with series such as *The Avengers* and *The Saint* becoming global hits that still have cult status today.

In 1969 the studios were to come under the ownership of EMI and a year later MGM (Metro-Goldwyn Mayer) signed a partnership and the studios became known as EMI-MGM Elstree Studios for three years. Of course, the studios were home to all three *On the Buses* spin-off films from 1971 to 1973. Other comedy spin-off films were produced, as were a string of classic Hammer horror films. Having reverted to being known as EMI Elstree Studios, a big blockbuster was to come out of the studios in 1976. *Star Wars* hit the world and was a massive hit globally and remains one of the greatest science fiction films ever made. Other hit films continued to roll out of the studios into the early 1980s such as *The Shining* and the Indiana Jones Trilogy of films, with more stages also being built. However, dark days lay ahead for the famous old studios.

Thorn EMI sold the studios in 1986 to The Cannon Group but that company was already financially-stretched and Cannon were soon to sell off the Pathé news archive at Elstree and in 1988 the Brent Walker Group bought Elstree Studios. The future for the studios became decidedly uncertain as the new owners were a renowned property development group who applied for permission to redevelop a large portion of the studios site which was granted. The bulldozers moved in to 12 acres of the studio site as a campaign dubbed 'Save Our Studios' was set up, spearheaded by film historian and Borehamwood resident Paul Welsh. With a Tesco superstore replacing a large swathe of where the studios once stood and the remainder of the studios largely neglected, with equipment being sold off, things looked bleak. The campaign to save the studios saw it take on The Brent Walker Group and in 1993, in an incredible turnaround, the studios were saved from destruction when Brent Walker settled out of court and Hertsmere Borough Council took over ownership of the remainder of the studios.

The studios were slowly refurbished and re-opened in 1999 and since then the Elstree Studios have sprung very much back into life. The facilities are now profitable and have churned out smash hit films including *World War Z*, *The King's Speech* and *Paddington*. Also, hit television series such as *Big Brother*, *Who Wants to be a Millionaire?*, *Strictly Come Dancing*, *Pointless* and *Never Mind the Buzzcocks* have come out of Elstree and the story is set to go on. The studios are undergoing large-scale redevelopment to increase the site in size and facilities and the future looks bright for Elstree Studios, often dubbed Britain's Hollywood.

How to get there: The most direct route to this location is via train from London St Pancras Station (Lower Level) aboard a Thameslink service to Elstree and Borehamwood Station. Exit Elstree and Borehamwood Station and from Stop A board the No. 107 bus (to New Barnet) or the No. 292 bus (to Colindale). Disembark at the undesignated stop (Elstree Studios) which is four stops into your journey and across the road to your left stands Elstree Studios.

Now

Elstree Studios as it looks today.

Location 91: Stan and Jack Ogle a Clippie

Film: *On the Buses*

Tesco Superstore, Shenley Road, Borehamwood, Hertfordshire, WD6 1JG.

In the opening scene of the first spin-off film, *On the Buses* (18 seconds into the film), we see a bus parked outside the bus depot and a clippie is precariously positioned changing the destination boards on the bus. Stan and Jack arrive on the scene to offer advice which is more beneficial to them than her. This scene was filmed on the backlot at Elstree Studios with the large Stage 5 structure being used for external and internal shots of the bus depot in all three spin-off films. Sadly, this portion of the studios were demolished and replaced in the early 1990s by a Tesco Extra superstore, which still stands on the site to this day and the double doors into Stage 5 would have stood where the glass-covered walkway leading up to Tesco through the car park stands now.

How to get there: The most direct route to this location is via train from London St Pancras Station (Lower Level) aboard a Thameslink service to Elstree and Borehamwood Station. Exit Elstree and Borehamwood Station and from Stop A board the No. 107 bus (to New Barnet) or the No. 292 bus (to Colindale). Disembark at the undesignated stop (Borehamwood Tesco) which is three stops into your journey. Turn right and walk through the car park for 75 metres to the Tesco Extra to where Stage 5 stood.

Then

Now

The canopied walkway to Tesco is very close to where the entrance into Stage 5 stood.

Location 92: Opening Credits – On the Buses

Film: *On the Buses*

Shenley Road, Borehamwood, Hertfordshire, WD6 1AD.

The opening credits of *On the Buses* begin to role (2 minutes 57 seconds into the film) and a bus can be seen travelling down a busy high street. On the left is a row of shops and to the right is a grand looking post office with large arched windows. This scene was filmed on Shenley Road – the main street that runs through the heart of Borehamwood, which was no more than half a mile away from the Elstree Studios where the film was made. The location today has had one or two cosmetic changes, with the zebra crossing outside the post office in the film no longer being there today, whilst the road has been narrowed somewhat by the addition of a central reservation.

How to get there: The most direct route to this location is via train from London St Pancras Station (Lower Level) aboard a Thameslink service to Elstree and Borehamwood Station. Exit Elstree and Borehamwood Station, turn left and walk for 55 metres before crossing Station Road and onto Shenley Road. Walk 75 metres eastwards along Shenley Road and directly across the road on your left is the post office seen in the opening credits.

Then

Now

The former post office building on the right behind the To Let sign.

Location 93: Opening Credits – Not Stopping for Passengers

Film: *On the Buses*

Rossington Avenue, Borehamwood, Hertfordshire, WD6 4LA.

As the opening credits of *On the Buses* continue to roll, Stan drives his bus up a suburban street (3 minutes 10 seconds into the film) and as he drives his bus past a bus stop with waiting passengers he yells: "Full up!" This scene was filmed on Rossington Avenue with the bus stop on the pavement directly outside No. 76 Rossington Avenue. Today this location remains much the same although a number of properties adjacent to the bus stop have undergone extensions to their properties and had cosmetic refurbishments.

How to get there: The most direct route to this location is via train from London St Pancras Station (Lower Level) aboard a Thameslink service to Elstree and Borehamwood Station. Exit Elstree and Borehamwood Station and from Stop C board the No. 292 bus (to Rossington Avenue). Disembark at the terminating stop (Rossington Avenue) and turn right to cross Rossington Avenue. Then turn left and walk 45 metres to No. 76 Rossington Avenue where the bus stop was located on the pavement outside that property.

Then

Now

The bus stop stood where there is now a tree in the foreground.

Location 94: Opening Credits – Introducing Mum and Arthur

Film: *On the Buses*

Rossington Avenue, Borehamwood, Hertfordshire, WD6 4LA.

Stan's bus pulls up outside a small row of shops and his mum waits to board as the opening credits of *On the Buses* continue and she calls to Arthur who stands next to a grocery shop door (3 minutes 39 seconds into the film). This shop has a wooden-framed window with the windows angled in towards the shop door in the centre of the property. This shop remains to this day and is located on Rossington Avenue but is now a hairdressing salon. However, the exterior of the salon does remain much the same with the wooden-framed windows still present, making it easy to identify.

How to get there: The most direct route to this location is via train from London St Pancras Station (Lower Level) aboard a Thameslink service to Elstree and Borehamwood Station. Exit Elstree and Borehamwood Station and from Stop C board the No. 292 bus (to Rossington Avenue). Disembark at the terminating stop (Rossington Avenue) and turn right to cross Rossington Avenue to the row of shops with the hairdressing salon at No. 44 being seen in this scene.

Then

Now

Arthur stood to the left and Mum to the right of this shop door.

Location 95: Opening Credits – Introducing Blakey

Film: *On the Buses*

Thirsk Road, Borehamwood, Hertfordshire, WD6 5AX.

The opening credits introduce Blakey in a scene that sees a bus travel down a road with a decline in it as the inspector stands by a bus stop with a big puddle in front of him (4 minutes 24 seconds into the film). Behind him are a row of houses with distinctive balconies on the second floor of these properties, whilst across the road was an area of overgrown grassland. This scene was filmed in Thirsk Road with Blakey standing approximately on the pavement outside No. 40 Thirsk Road. The location today remains fairly similar with some of the properties having undergone refurbishment and the grassland on the opposite side of the road has partially been redeveloped with new properties present, whilst the remaining grassland area now has a greater population of trees. If you visit this location, the point of the metal plate at the edge of the pavement drain is where Blakey stood and ends up being splashed. This scene was virtually recreated (with a twist) in the opening credits of *Mutiny on the Buses*.

How to get there: The most direct route to this location is via train from London St Pancras Station (Lower Level) aboard a Thameslink service to Elstree and Borehamwood Station. Exit Elstree and Borehamwood Station and from Stop A board the No. 306 Sullivan Buses service (to Watford High Street). Disembark at the undesignated stop (Thirsk Road) and second stop on Stanborough Avenue, turn left onto a path and walk for 50 metres until reaching Thirsk Road. Turn left and walk 45 metres to the pavement outside the communal entry to Nos. 36 to 42 Thirsk Road where Blakey stood for this scene.

Then

Now

The curving and dipping road where Blakey gets splashed.

Then

Now

**The view behind Blakey after being splashed has
changed very little with the balcony in centre of shot
seen directly behind him in the film.**

Location 96: Opening Credits – Introducing Jack

Film: *On the Buses*

Cardinal Avenue, Borehamwood, Hertfordshire, WD6 1ER.

With the *On the Buses* film's opening credits still rolling we see Stan's bus turn a corner and stopping to pick up passengers. Jack eyes up an attractive blonde as she goes upstairs before he rings the bell for the bus to depart (4 minutes 35 seconds into the film). The bus is seen travelling eastwards along Whitehouse Avenue before turning into Cardinal Avenue in Borehamwood. The bus stop was located directly outside No. 62 Cardinal Avenue and from the mound of earth at the base of the bus stop I'd say most definitely it was an artificial bus stop. The properties at this location have undergone cosmetic changes but the general layout remains much the same.

How to get there: The most direct route to this location is via train from London St Pancras Station (Lower Level) aboard a Thameslink service to Elstree and Borehamwood Station. Exit Elstree and Borehamwood Station, turn left and walk for 55 metres before crossing Station Road and onto Shenley Road. Walk 335 metres eastwards along Shenley Road and turn right into Cardinal Avenue, then walk 150 metres to the pavement outside No. 62 Cardinal Avenue where this scene was filmed.

Then

Now

Jack was introduced in the opening credits here in the first spin-off film in 1971.

Location 97: Opening Credits – Roy Skeggs

Film: *On the Buses*

Shenley Road, Borehamwood, Hertfordshire, WD6 1EF.

Continuing on with the opening credits in the *On the Buses* film, Stan's bus travels down a main street flanked by shops on either side of the road (5 minutes 18 seconds into the film) before turning right into a side street. This scene was filmed on the stretch of Shenley Road shortly after the left turn into Cardinal Avenue and up to the turn into Whitehouse Avenue where the bus is seen turning into. The main changes to this, which is the main street in Borehamwood, is that a central reservation now runs up the centre of the road, narrowing it a great deal, and obviously the shops on either side are now under new ownership.

How to get there: The most direct route to this location is via train from London St Pancras Station (Lower Level) aboard a Thameslink service to Elstree and Borehamwood Station. Exit Elstree and Borehamwood Station, turn left and walk for 55 metres before crossing Station Road and onto Shenley Road. Walk 400 metres eastwards along Shenley Road and roughly adjacent to No. 122 Shenley Road is where the bus passes at the above time in the film.

Then

Now

Stan's bus travels towards the camera as the opening credits rolls.

Location 98: Opening Credits – The Butler House

Film: *On the Buses*

Malden Road, Borehamwood, Hertfordshire, WD6 1BW.

Stan's bus turns into a narrow street as the opening credits to the first spin-off film continue and his family get off with their shopping and head into their house (6 minutes 2 seconds into the film). The Butler house (which is seen many times in all three spin-off films) is located at No. 2 Malden Road. Today the property remains but there have been cosmetic changes. The red-bricked frontage has been replaced by whitewashed bricks and the small garden wall around the front of the property has now been removed. To the immediate left of the property, now a cul-de-sac, new properties have been built on what was wasteland. If you visit this location, note the false railway bridge to the left of the property which is the bridge on the *EastEnders* set.

How to get there: The most direct route to this location is via train from London St Pancras Station (Lower Level) aboard a Thameslink service to Elstree and Borehamwood Station. Exit Elstree and Borehamwood Station, turn left and walk for 55 metres before crossing Station Road and onto Shenley Road. Cross Shenley Road and walk 290 metres eastwards along Shenley Road before turning left into Clarendon Road. Walk 200 metres and directly ahead is No. 2 Malden Road – the Butler house.

Then

Now

The Butler residence seen in all three spin-off films.

Location 99: Opening Credits – Approaching Turnaround Point

Film: *On the Buses*

Whitehouse Avenue, Borehamwood, Hertfordshire, WD6 1HA.

As the opening credits of *On the Buses* approach their end (6 minutes 4 seconds into the film) Stan's bus travels up a residential street towards its fictional Town's End turnaround point of its journey. In the distance a main street can be seen at the end of the road and on either side of the bus are houses of varying architecture with a mix of bungalows and semi-detached houses. The bus was filmed travelling south on Whitehouse Avenue, which remains much the same to the present day and the main road seen at the end of the street is Shenley Road. The camera would have filmed this brief scene looking northwards from the pavement outside No. 19 Whitehouse Avenue and it was at this same location where the bus shelter is demolished by Stan.

How to get there: The most direct route to this location is via train from London St Pancras Station (Lower Level) aboard a Thameslink service to Elstree and Borehamwood Station. Exit Elstree and Borehamwood Station, turn left and walk for 55 metres before crossing Station Road and onto Shenley Road. Walk 335 metres eastwards along Shenley Road and turn right into Whitehouse Avenue. Cross the road, turn right and walk 100 metres. On your left is a semi-circular wall outside Nos. 17 and 19 Whitehouse Avenue where the camera would have filmed this scene looking northwards towards Shenley Road.

Then

Now

Stan's bus approaching the turnaround point as the opening credits near their end.

Location 100: Turnaround Betty's House

Film: *On the Buses*

Whitehouse Avenue, Borehamwood, Hertfordshire, WD6 1HD.

With Stan having parked his bus at the turnaround point, Jack prepares to head across the road to a waiting housewife clad in a scanty nightgown (6 minutes 24 seconds into the film). This location is seen frequently throughout the first spin-off film and Turnaround Betty's house was No. 20 Whitehouse Avenue. The house remains fairly unchanged to the present day, aside from new windows being fitted, repainted brickwork, the garden wall being removed and, remarkably, the famous washing line remains as well. It is almost certain that the interior of the house was used for filming as we get a view looking down to the street below so cameras clearly accessed the bedroom for this shot. However, the bedroom scenes were filmed at the studios, as the view out of the window of the property opposite does not match-up with the actual property across the road from No 20. Whitehouse Avenue.

How to get there: The most direct route to this location is via train from London St Pancras Station (Lower Level) aboard a Thameslink service to Elstree and Borehamwood Station. Exit Elstree and Borehamwood Station, turn left and walk for 55 metres before crossing Station Road and onto Shenley Road. Walk 335 metres eastwards along Shenley Road and turn right into Whitehouse Avenue. Walk 100 metres and on your right is No. 20 Whitehouse Avenue – Turnaround Betty's house.

Then

Now

Turnaround Betty's house which features in several scenes in the first spin-off film.

Location 101: The Family Planning Clinic

Film: *On the Buses*

Shenley Road, Borehamwood, Hertfordshire, WD6 1JG.

As Stan's bus stops, Olive is seen getting off the bus and Jack points her in the direction of the family planning clinic and she heads off towards it (21 minutes 45 seconds into the film). The family planning clinic was actually once the studio manager's house on the grounds of Elstree Studios on Shenley Road, which at that time was being used for administration purposes. This house has since been demolished and where it once stood is the western most end of the car park of Elstree Studios, near three plaques which stand on a grass verge paying homage to the town's rich history in the film production industry. Directly across the road in the film was a roadside sign which remains today and the Studio 70 cinema which has long since been demolished to be replaced by office blocks, which in turn are currently awaiting redevelopment. A roundabout replaces a straight stretch of road in the film.

How to get there: The most direct route to this location is via train from London St Pancras Station (Lower Level) aboard a Thameslink service to Elstree and Borehamwood Station. Exit Elstree and Borehamwood Station and from Stop A board the No. 107 bus (to New Barnet) or the No. 292 bus (to Colindale). Disembark at the undesignated stop (Elstree Studios) which is four stops into your journey. Turn left, walk 15 metres and turn left to cross Shenley Road. Directly ahead you will see three plaques and beyond these is approximately where the family planning clinic stood.

Then

Now

The road sign to the far left can be seen in the film and to the far right where we see bushes is where the Family Planning Clinic sign stood.

Location 102: Approaching the Launderette

Film: *On the Buses*

Manor Way, Borehamwood, Hertfordshire, WD6 1QR.

Stan's bus approaches a bus stop as he intends on making a quick visit to drop off his laundry at the launderette (28 minutes 34 seconds into the film). On either side of the road are houses, whilst directly across the road from the bus stop is a church. This scene was filmed on Manor Way with the bus stop located on the pavement directly outside No. 87 Manor Way. Today the location remains much the same with the grassy verges by the roadside still present although the paving slabs on the pavements have been replaced. This bus stop is seen later when Blakey stands there and sees Stan's bus stopping outside the launderette with the circular manhole cover still present there to this day.

How to get there: The most direct route to this location is via train from London St Pancras Station (Lower Level) aboard a Thameslink service to Elstree and Borehamwood Station. Exit Elstree and Borehamwood Station and from Stop A board the No. 292 bus (to Colindale). Disembark at the undesignated stop (Ripon Park) and turn left and walk 230 metres along Manor Way until reaching the pavement where the bus stop stood outside No. 87 Manor Way.

Then

Now

The bus stop that the passengers wait at stood just across the other side of the small side road on the right.

Location 103: Stopping at the Launderette

Film: *On the Buses*

Manor Way, Borehamwood, Hertfordshire, WD6 1QX.

Seconds later, Stan's bus passes the bus stop without stopping, then comes to a halt moments later (28 minutes 44 seconds into the film). He jumps out of his cab and runs across the road with a laundry bag to the launderette opposite. This launderette is still located at No. 120 Manor Way although it has changed its shop sign since then, probably numerous times. The pavements are also now covered by ornate brickwork outside the launderette replacing the paving slabs. This particular road was used in several scenes in the spin-off films and the launderette features later in the film from a different angle.

How to get there: The most direct route to this location is via train from London St Pancras Station (Lower Level) aboard a Thameslink service to Elstree and Borehamwood Station. Exit Elstree and Borehamwood Station and from Stop A board the No. 292 bus (to Colindale). Disembark at the undesignated stop (Ripon Park) and turn left and walk 210 metres along Manor Way. On your left across the road is the launderette that features in this film.

Then

Now

The launderette today with parked cars and vans much more prevalent today than in 1971.

Location 104: The Knicker-Snatcher Scene

Film: *On the Buses*

Manor Way, Borehamwood, Hertfordshire, WD6 1QX.

When Stan has been caught by Blakey picking up a laundry bag outside the launderette he confiscates the bag, but two women accost the inspector and accuse him of being a knicker-snatcher before a policeman arrives to settle the dispute (31 minutes 9 seconds into the film). In this scene, filmed outside the launderette on Manor Way, the camera looks southwards up Manor Way with the long line of shops on one side of the road. Further up on the same side of the road was a small residential block of flats which also still remain there today.

How to get there: The most direct route to this location is via train from London St Pancras Station (Lower Level) aboard a Thameslink service to Elstree and Borehamwood Station. Exit Elstree and Borehamwood Station and from Stop A board the No. 292 bus (to Colindale). Disembark at the undesignated stop (Ripon Park) and turn left and walk 210 metres along Manor Way. Turn left and cross the road to the point on the pavement where Stan's bus parked for this scene and look south for the view seen by the camera.

Then

Now

Stan and Jack revelled in the inspector's discomfort but today the space is taken up by parked cars.

Location 105: The Skidpan Scene

Film: *On the Buses*

Chiswick Business Park, Chiswick High Road, London, W4 5YA.

Stan is forced to pass a test on London Transport's skidpan facility after demolishing a telephone booth and bus shelter. He mischievously decides to take the test whilst Blakey is still aboard. The inspector finds it a rough ride (46 minutes 29 seconds into the film) and in the background we can see a row of houses and the side of a small residential block of flats. This scene was filmed at London Transport's skidpan at Chiswick which was used to test and train their drivers, but sadly it closed in 1987 and was to be demolished and replaced by a massive business park. The road that runs down the east side of the business park is roughly where Stan's bus is seen as it is about to make its second run on the test. The skidpan was located on Chiswick High Road and, although no trace is left of the facility, the photograph below shows the stretch of Chiswick High Road seen in the background as Blakey clings to the rear of the bus. If you intend on visiting this location then, before taking photographs on the grounds of the Chiswick Business Park, head to Building Three on the site and from reception ask for a pass allowing you to take photographs and explain the reason you wish to take photographs.

How to get there: The most direct route to this location is via tube from Victoria Station on the District Line heading westbound to Gunnersbury Station. Exit Gunnersbury Station and cross Chiswick High Road at the level crossing. Turn right and walk 10 metres before crossing at the entrance into the Chiswick Business Park. Turn left and walk 25 metres before turning right to walk along a path in front of an office block. Walk 65 metres to the end of the path and you will reach the area roughly where my photograph was taken if you turn to look right onto Chiswick High Road.

By bus the most direct route is from Stop F outside Paddington Station aboard the No. 27 bus (to Chiswick Business Park). Disembark at the terminus at Chiswick Business Park, turn left and walk 165 metres down the road on the east side of the business park. Turn right to cross the zebra crossing. Walk 90 metres and turn left on passing the office block on your left, then walk a further 60 metres passing two office blocks on your left. Finally, turn left to walk along a path in front of an office block. Walk 65 metres to the end of the path and you will reach the area roughly where my photograph was taken if you turn to look right onto Chiswick High Road.

Then

**The two buildings on the horizon in the distance are
379 Chiswick High Road on the left and the side-on view
of the Gunnersbury Close residential flats on the right.**

Now

**The view of Chiswick High Road today seen as Blakey
hangs on to the back of the bus.**

Location 106: False Diversions Await

Film: *On the Buses*

Wetherby Road, Borehamwood, Hertfordshire, WD6 4LH.

A bus driven by Ruby is about to start following false diversion signs placed strategically by Stan and Jack. Her bus makes its way down a narrow residential street (51 minutes 17 seconds into the film) before turning right down another street lined by houses. This was filmed with the bus shot travelling from the west end of Wetherby Road in the north of Borehamwood before turning right into Cromwell Road. Today the location remains virtually unchanged though a number of garden hedges have been removed allowing owners to use their front gardens as parking space for their cars.

How to get there: The most direct route to this location is via train from London St Pancras Station (Lower Level) aboard a Thameslink service to Elstree and Borehamwood Station. Exit Elstree and Borehamwood Station and from Stop A board the No. 398 Sullivan Buses service (to Watford). Disembark at the stop (opposite Wetherby Road), turn left and walk 10 metres along Theobald Street, turn left to cross the zebra crossing and walk ten metres straight ahead onto Wetherby Road. After a further 40-metre walk turn right into Cromwell Road. Cross the road and walk approximately 15 metres and turn to face Wetherby Road for the angle the camera filmed this scene.

Then

Now

The view from Cromwell Road where the bus takes a right-hand turn out of Wetherby Road.

Location 107: The First Diversion Sign

Film: *On the Buses*

Gateshead Road, Borehamwood, Hertfordshire, WD6 5LJ.

Ruby drives her bus up a narrow street lined by houses and ahead of her is an adjacent street with a diversion sign attached to a lamp post (51 minutes 25 seconds into the film). She follows the sign, turning left. This part of the scene was filmed with the bus heading out of Stanborough Avenue and turning left into Gateshead Road in North Borehamwood with a row of red-bricked houses in the background, those being Nos. 244 and 246. This location has remained much the same today with the lamp post still present but of a more modern design. The houses have had double-glazed windows, replacing the old design and the hedges running along the front of the properties have largely been removed.

How to get there: The most direct route to this location is via train from London St Pancras Station (Lower Level) aboard a Thameslink service to Elstree and Borehamwood Station. Exit Elstree and Borehamwood Station and from Stop A board the No. 306 Sullivan Buses service (to Borehamwood Tesco). Disembark at the undesignated stop (adjacent to Reston Path) on Gateshead Road, turn right and walk 180 metres until reaching the junction with Stanborough Avenue. Cross Stanborough Avenue and look right to Nos. 244 and 246 Gateshead Road seen in the film.

Then

Now

**The first diversion sign was attached to an older design
of lamp post that stood here.**

Location 108: Following the First Diversion Sign

Film: *On the Buses*

Cromwell Road, Borehamwood, Hertfordshire, WD6 4LJ.

On seeing the first diversion sign, Ruby's bus turns sharply left down a narrow street and mounts the pavement (51 minutes 31 seconds into the film) with white-washed houses lining either side of the road. This scene was filmed with the bus heading south down Cromwell Road and the camera would have filmed this scene roughly outside No. 34 Cromwell Road as the bus heads towards it. The houses today have lost their whitewashed appearances and they have either returned to their red or have painted tan brickwork.

How to get there: The most direct route to this location is via train from London St Pancras Station (Lower Level) aboard a Thameslink service to Elstree and Borehamwood Station. Exit Elstree and Borehamwood Station and from Stop A board the No. 398 Sullivan Buses service (to Watford). Disembark at the stop (opposite Wetherby Road), turn left and walk 10 metres along Theobald Street. Turn left to cross the zebra crossing and walk ten metres straight ahead onto Wetherby Road. After a further 40-metre walk turn right into Cromwell Road. Cross the road and walk approximately 115 metres to the pavement outside No. 34 Cromwell Road and turn to look north for the angle seen in the film.

Then

Now

The houses lining this street look far different today with brickwork replacing the whitewashed houses.

Location 109: The Second Diversion Sign

Film: *On the Buses*

Cromwell Road, Borehamwood, Hertfordshire, WD6 4LN.

As Ruby continues to drive her bus down a narrow street she sees a second diversion sign attached to a lamp post, turns left (51 minutes 37 seconds into the film) and soon realises her error. In the final part of this scene Ruby's bus travels down Cromwell Road with the diversion sign on a lamp post outside No. 49 Cromwell Road before turning left, continuing along the same road. The properties in this area remain largely unchanged aside from some garden hedges being removed and a slight repositioning of a telegraph pole and a lamp post but thankfully not the one which had the diversion sign attached to it.

How to get there: The most direct route to this location is via train from London St Pancras Station (Lower Level) aboard a Thameslink service to Elstree and Borehamwood Station. Exit Elstree and Borehamwood Station and from Stop C board the No. 292 bus (to Rossington Avenue). Disembark at the undesignated stop (Cromwell Road) on Rossington Avenue and turn right, walking 5 metres before turning left into Cromwell Road. Walk 45 metres and cross the road to the pavement outside No. 28 Cromwell Road where the camera looked westwards in filming the bus rounding the corner.

Then

Now

The second diversion sign was at this location and the houses in the background have remained much the same.

Then

Now

**Moments later the bus turns a corner with the camera
filming this scene from the pavement outside No. 28
Cromwell Road.**

Location 110: The Third Diversion Sign

Film: *On the Buses*

Cromwell Road, Borehamwood, Hertfordshire, WD6 4LW.

There is a third and last diversion sign for Ruby to pass in her bus and this is attached to another lamp post (51 minutes 50 seconds into the film) further down the road. This lamp post remains to this day but is of newer design and has been moved a few metres to the west, just outside No. 25 Cromwell Road. The only real differences to this location today are that many of the garden hedges have been removed allowing cars to be parked in the front gardens of the properties and many houses have been fitted with double-glazed windows.

How to get there: The most direct route to this location is via train from London St Pancras Station (Lower Level) aboard a Thameslink service to Elstree and Borehamwood Station. Exit Elstree and Borehamwood Station and from Stop C board the No. 292 bus (to Rossington Avenue). Disembark at the undesignated stop (Cromwell Road) on Rossington Avenue and turn right, walking 5 metres before turning left into Cromwell Road. Walk 85 metres and you will reach the lamp post with the third diversion sign attached.

Then

Now

The third diversion sign scene was shot here.

Location 111: A Bus with Spiders Aboard

Film: *On the Buses*

Leeming Road, Borehamwood, Hertfordshire, WD6 4EB.

Vera's bus, with a number of spiders in her cab, makes its way along a street lined by shops (54 minutes 20 seconds into the film) with a small block of flats in the background. This was filmed in Leeming Road in Borehamwood with the bus heading southwards. In the present day the location has changed very little. The road has been narrowed to allow for car parking space, a zebra crossing is now in place and obviously the shops are under new ownership. The bus is seen passing what is now a café, called Marco's, on the left of Leeming Road.

How to get there: The most direct route to this location is via train from London St Pancras Station (Lower Level) aboard a Thameslink service to Elstree and Borehamwood Station. Exit Elstree and Borehamwood Station and from Stop C board the No. 292 bus (to Rossington Avenue). Disembark at the undesignated stop (Leeming Road) and turn right to walk 90 metres along Leeming Road. Turn right, cross at the zebra crossing and turn to look north up Leeming Road for the direction the bus approaches in the film.

Then

Now

Leeming Road in 2015, noticeably narrower than in 1971 and with more trees now lining the street.

Location 112: Itching Legs

Film: *On the Buses*

Gateshead Road, Borehamwood, Hertfordshire, WD6 5LJ.

As spiders begin to crawl up Vera's leg she itches as she drives her bus. The camera cuts to a brief exterior shot (54 minutes 32 seconds into the film) with the bus travelling along a slightly curved road on a decline with houses on either side of the road with grassy verges between the pavement and kerbs. This location would have been filmed with the bus heading east on Gateshead Road at the junction of Stanborough Avenue in Borehamwood. Today this location has minor differences with most of the grassy verges on the left side of the road gone, trees lining the road having grown somewhat and newer designed lamp posts replacing the older versions.

How to get there: The most direct route to this location is via train from London St Pancras Station (Lower Level) aboard a Thameslink service to Elstree and Borehamwood Station. Exit Elstree and Borehamwood Station and from Stop A board the No. 306 Sullivan Buses service (to Borehamwood Tesco). Disembark at the undesignated stop (Thirsk Road) and first stop on Stanborough Avenue, turn left and walk 60 metres until at the junction of Gateshead Road where this location was filmed.

Then

Now

Vera's bus travelled along this road moments before her crash.

Location 113: Swerving Bus

Film: *On the Buses*

Gateshead Road, Borehamwood, Hertfordshire, WD6 5DZ.

The itching for Vera becomes more intense and her bus is seen swerving as it goes down a road on an incline (54 minutes 43 seconds into the film). The bus heads west, passing an entrance to Grove Road which has a distinctively-shaped bungalow on an angle on the corner and a line of houses on the other side of Gateshead Road, with grassy verges prevalent and trees lining the road. The location remains much the same today with minor differences such as a few garden hedges being removed from properties.

How to get there: The most direct route to this location is via train from London St Pancras Station (Lower Level) aboard a Thameslink service to Elstree and Borehamwood Station. Exit Elstree and Borehamwood Station and from Stop A board the No. 306 Sullivan Buses service (to Borehamwood Tesco). Disembark at the undesignated stop (Digswell Close) on Gateshead Road, turn left and walk 50 metres to the pavement outside No. 181 Gateshead Road. Turn for the angle the camera would have had for shooting this scene.

Then

Now

The bus begins to swerve across the road at this location.

Location 114: Policeman Directs Traffic

Film: *On the Buses*

Gateshead Road, Borehamwood, Hertfordshire, WD6 5LZ.

A policeman standing in the middle of the road directs traffic (54 minutes 54 seconds into the film) at a junction. A long line of traffic queues along what was Gateshead Road to the west and the policeman stands at the entrance into Stanborough Avenue, releasing traffic from that road. This location remains much the same and even a crack in the road tarmac running the length of the entrance into Stanborough Avenue remains evident to this day. Grassy verges have reduced and newer lamp posts and trees having grown somewhat over the years, with a roundabout painted into the tarmac at the junction of Gateshead Road and Stanborough Avenue the only notable differences. This scene would have been filmed with the camera fixed on the corner of Stanborough Avenue and Gateshead Road (near No. 269) looking west. Seconds later, this location is seen again from the same angle when the policeman is knocked off his feet by a dumper truck.

How to get there: The most direct route to this location is via train from London St Pancras Station (Lower Level) aboard a Thameslink service to Elstree and Borehamwood Station. Exit Elstree and Borehamwood Station and from Stop A board the No. 306 Sullivan Buses service (to Borehamwood Tesco). Disembark at the undesignated stop (Thirsk Road) and first stop on Stanborough Avenue, turn left and walk 60 metres until at the junction of Gateshead Road, turn left, cross Stanborough Avenue and walk 5 metres east on Gateshead Road where this location was filmed looking west.

Then

Now

**The policeman directed traffic here and the cracked
tarmac still remains in the road.**

Location 115: Bus Continues to Swerve

Film: *On the Buses*

Gateshead Road, Borehamwood, Hertfordshire, WD6 5LL.

As the itching continues for Vera, the bus continues to swerve as it passes a road on the left (54 minutes 55 seconds into the film) and the road declines quite sharply with houses on either side of the road. The bus is filmed heading west down Gateshead Road and the road on the left is Aycliffe Road, identifiable by the slight angle of the house on the corner and the large sloping grassy bank in front of it which is still there today. A roundabout has now been painted onto the tarmac at the junction of Aycliffe Road and Gateshead Road. The bus is seen just passing No. 176 Gateshead Road which is to the far right and out of shot.

How to get there: The most direct route to this location is via train from London St Pancras Station (Lower Level) aboard a Thameslink service to Elstree and Borehamwood Station. Exit Elstree and Borehamwood Station and from Stop A board the No. 306 Sullivan Buses service (to Borehamwood Tesco). Disembark at the undesignated stop (Digswell Close) on Gateshead Road, turn right, walk 85 metres and cross the road where you are adjacent to No. 176 Gateshead Road, where the bus is passing as it heads westwards in this scene.

Then

Now

Vera's bus was filmed travelling down this street an instant before her crash.

Location 116: Bus Crashes into Truck

Film: *On the Buses*

Stanborough Avenue, Borehamwood, Hertfordshire, WD6 5LP.

Moments before crashing her bus into the back of a truck, Vera lets out a scream and we get a view of the road ahead (55 minutes and 1 second into the film). The truck ahead stands on Stanborough Avenue at the junction of Gateshead Road and the bus crashes into the rear of the truck on the stretch of the road outside No. 2 Stanborough Avenue. Seconds later in the film, we see the same camera angle again as the policeman gets to his feet and walks towards a panicking Vera and Inspector Blake. The only noticeable differences to this location are the newer design of lamp posts in place and the roundabout painted on the road at the junction of Stanborough Avenue and Gateshead Road, which was not present in the film.

How to get there: The most direct route to this location is via train from London St Pancras Station (Lower Level) aboard a Thameslink service to Elstree and Borehamwood Station. Exit Elstree and Borehamwood Station and from Stop A board the No. 306 Sullivan Buses service (to Borehamwood Tesco). Disembark at the undesignated stop (Thirsk Road) and first stop on Stanborough Avenue, turn left, walk 50 metres, turn left and cross Stanborough Avenue to the pavement outside No. 2 which is roughly the stretch of road where the bus crashes into the truck.

Then

Now

The truck that Vera's bus crashes into was parked here.

Location 117: Toilet Stop at a Garage

Film: *On the Buses*

St Albans Road, South Mimms, Hertfordshire, EN6 3PN.

A bus speeds along a road lined by houses (64 minutes and 9 seconds into the film) and turns quickly right into a garage. The driver, Ada, rushes out of her cab to a toilet after drinking tea laced with diuretic pills. This scene was filmed on St Albans Road on the outskirts of the town of Potters Bar. A garage remains to this day on the site but had been greatly refurbished before closing for business in recent times, whilst the street signpost Brookside remains but has been slightly repositioned. The houses that the bus passes remain to this day and are largely unchanged although they have been repainted a brighter colour replacing the pebble-dashing exteriors and the hedge along the side of the house next to the garage (No. 26 St Albans Road) has been partially replaced by a wooden fence.

How to get there: The most direct route to this location is via train from London King's Cross Station aboard a Great Northern service to Potters Bar. Exit Potters Bar Station and from Stop B board the No. 398 Sullivan Buses service (to Watford Town Centre). Disembark at the undesignated stop (opposite The White Hart), turn left and walk four metres to the point where Ada's bus pulls into the garage on your right. Note the Brookside signpost seen in the film directly ahead.

Then

Now

Ada's bus pulls into this garage in the film but today the garage has closed for business.

Location 118: Two Buses at one Public Toilet

Film: *On the Buses*

Park Street Lane, St Albans, Hertfordshire, AL2 2NE.

A block of public toilets are seen (64 minutes 18 seconds into the film) and two buses screech to a halt, stopping inches apart as the two desperate women bus drivers rush to get to the toilets – another two victims of drinking tea laced with diuretic pills. These public toilets are located on Park Street Lane in St Albans and remain in service to the current day. This location remains virtually unaltered aside from the front of the toilets being painted cream whereas they were dark green in the film. All surrounding buildings remain refreshingly unchanged apart from that.

How to get there: The most direct route to this location is via train from London Euston aboard a London Midland service to Watford Junction. Disembark at Watford Junction and board another London Midland service to Park Street Station. Exit Park Street Station, walk 20 metres onto Watling Street and turn left. Walk 440 metres, turn right into Park Lane Street and walk 40 metres. To your left directly across the road are the public toilets seen in the film.

Then

Now

Ruby and Vera fight to reach the toilet first here in 1971.

Location 119: Toilet in a Public House

Film: *On the Buses*

London Road, Shenley, Hertfordshire, WD7 9ER.

Ruby exits a toilet located in the backyard of a public house (64 minutes 31 seconds into the film) only to see an old man watering plants, which urges her to rush back into the toilet. This scene was filmed on the grounds of The White Horse public house in the village of Shenley. The outdoor drinking area remains but the seven-foot high wooden fence surrounding it has been replaced by a smaller and less enclosed metal fence. The large tree by the toilet door remains and has grown somewhat, but the door has been replaced and the exterior of the public house is now a mint green colour rather than cream as seen in the film.

How to get there: The most direct route to this location is via train from London St Pancras Station (Lower Level) aboard a Thameslink service to Elstree and Borehamwood Station. Exit Elstree and Borehamwood Station and from Stop B board the No. 658 Uno service (to St Albans). Disembark at the undesignated stop (The White Horse) on London Road and turn left. Walk 70 metres and turn right into the outdoor drinking area of The White Horse pub where this scene was filmed.

Then

Now

The tree still remains but note the door Ruby exits from has been replaced, although you can see where the door once stood.

Then

Now

The grass has been replaced by a concrete surfaced seating area with tables and chairs with the high wooden fence also gone.

Location 120: Country Lane Toilet Stop

Film: *On the Buses*

London Road, Shenley, Hertfordshire, WD6 5PH.

A bus travels along a country lane and pulls to a stop on the roadside (64 minutes 46 seconds into the film) and a moment later Peggy climbs out of her driver's cab. She dashes to some bushes to her left in a desperate need for the toilet, where a parson upstairs on her bus sees more than he bargained for. This scene was filmed on London Road at the entrance to Crossoaks Farm just over half a mile south of the village of Shenley. The clues to this location are the three telegraph poles on the left of the road, the positions of the trees and the curve in the road in the distance. Today, the only difference is that the entrance into Crossoaks Farm is now a concrete road instead of a dirt track as it was in 1971 and the trees along the roadside have grown somewhat in the ensuing years.

How to get there: The most direct route to this location is via train from London St Pancras Station (Lower Level) aboard a Thameslink service to Elstree and Borehamwood Station. Exit Elstree and Borehamwood Station and from Stop B board the No. 658 Uno service (to St Albans). Disembark at the undesignated stop (The White Horse) on London Road and turn left. Walk 1100 metres along London Road, heading south until reaching the entrance to Crossoaks Farm. Cross to the Crossoaks Farm entrance and look south for the direction the bus travels, stopping at the telegraph pole adjacent to where you stand.

Then

Now

Peggy's bus parks by the telegraph pole to the far right.

Location 121: A Trip to Hospital for a Check-up

Film: *On the Buses*

Leeming Road, Borehamwood, Hertfordshire, WD6 4DY.

Shortly after leaving home aboard the motorbike and sidecar, Arthur and Stan with Olive in the sidecar turn right out of a street lined with shops (67 minutes 26 seconds into the film). This scene filmed the motorbike heading northwards to turn out of Leeming Road and into Aycliffe Road. Aside from the shops having changed ownership, the paving slabs being replaced by a brickwork-surfaced pavement and Aycliffe Road being narrowed somewhat, this location remains much the same to the present day.

How to get there: The most direct route to this location is via train from London St Pancras Station (Lower Level) aboard a Thameslink service to Elstree and Borehamwood Station. Exit Elstree and Borehamwood Station and from Stop C board the No. 292 bus (to Rossington Avenue). Disembark at the undesignated stop (Baldock Way), turn left to walk 90 metres along Aycliffe Road and turn left to cross at the zebra crossing. Turn right, walk 25 metres and look right for the correct angle that the motorbike turns out of Leeming Road in the film.

Then

Now

Arthur's motorbike and sidecar turn right here on their way to the hospital.

Location 122: The Sidecar Problem

Film: *On the Buses*

London Road, Shenley, Hertfordshire, WD7 9DX.

As the trip to the hospital continues, Stan taps Arthur on the shoulder to bring his attention to the sidecar becoming loose (67 minutes 30 seconds into the film). The motorbike, at that time, is travelling southwards down a street in a village and this part of the scene was filmed in London Road, Shenley and follows them travelling just past the King William IV public house down as far as the Shenley Primary School and Nursery before cutting to the next location. This stretch of London Road remains very much unchanged I am pleased to say.

How to get there: The most direct route to this location is via train from London St Pancras Station (Lower Level) aboard a Thameslink service to Elstree and Borehamwood Station. Exit Elstree and Borehamwood Station and from Stop B board the No. 658 Uno service (to St Albans). Disembark at the undesignated stop (King William IV) on London Road, turn left and walk 20 metres to the zebra crossing. Cross here and turn right before walking 25 metres until just past the entry into Shenley Village Hall. Turn around for the direction the motorbike was filmed travelling.

Then

Now

Note the King William IV pub with the chimney stacks visible.

Location 123: Hasty Repairs

Film: *On the Buses*

Newcome Road, Shenley, Hertfordshire, WD7 9EG.

The motorbike comes to a halt on the corner of a quiet village street (67 minutes 43seconds into the film) and Stan tries to secure the sidecar by using wire as a makeshift solution. The motorbike halts and the street sign Newcome Road helps pinpoint this location. The house in the background is No. 38 Harris Lane in Shenley and still remains there today but has had an extension added to its west wing. It has been repainted and the small garden wall present in the film has been removed, but the hedge remains. The motorbike turns right here and continues down Harris Lane and you can note here that new pavements were about to be put in place as there is nothing but a sandy covering on the pavement to the right as the camera looks at it.

How to get there: The most direct route to this location is via train from London St Pancras Station (Lower Level) aboard a Thameslink service to Elstree and Borehamwood Station. Exit Elstree and Borehamwood Station and from Stop B board the No. 658 Uno service (to St Albans). Disembark at the undesignated stop (The White Horse) on London Road and turn right. Walk 65 metres, cross London Road and turn right into Harris Lane. Walk 130 metres, cross Harris Lane and on the pavement outside No. 19 Harris Lane is roughly where the camera would have filmed the motorbike stopping on the exit of Newcome Road.

Then

Now

The sidecar stops here for Stan to use wire to make the sidecar more secure.

Location 124: The Journey to Hospital Resumes

Film: *On the Buses*

Cowley Hill, Borehamwood, Hertfordshire, WD6 5ND.

The motorbike restarts its journey to the hospital and is seen travelling down a steep hill (68 minutes 36 seconds into the film) with houses on the right side of the road. To the left is a grassy verge with another road on the other side of that. This part of the scene was filmed looking southwards down Cowley Hill in Borehamwood and the bike is first seen passing No. 205 Cowley Hill before it turns right into Stapleton Road moments later, before taking a sharp turn left into Green Street and out of Borehamwood. This location has not changed too much at all aside from alterations to gardens on properties along Cowley Hill.

How to get there: The most direct route to this location is via train from London St Pancras Station (Lower Level) aboard a Thameslink service to Elstree and Borehamwood Station. Exit Elstree and Borehamwood Station and from Stop B board the No. 698 Uno service (to St Albans). Disembark at the undesignated stop (Stanborough Avenue) on Stapleton Road and turn and walk right for 60 metres along Stapleton Road. To your right is Cowley Hill where the motorbike is seen travelling down.

Then

Now

The old tree to the left of the area of grass has gone and a town sign stands there now.

Location 125: Along a Country Lane

Film: *On the Buses*

Wash Lane, Potters Bar, Hertfordshire, EN6 3QQ.

As the motorbike travels along a country lane lined by trees, the sidecar is seen having just rounded a bend with a small lane branching off in the background (68 minutes 50 seconds into the film). This scene was filmed on Wash Lane to the west of the town of Potters Bar. The location today has changed in that the road is no longer open to public traffic but the narrow road remains lined by trees on the left which have grown somewhat, with the grass verge on the right, although the road itself is in disrepair. The small lane branching off to our right remains and is just out of shot in the distance.

How to get there: The most direct route to this location is via train from London King's Cross Station aboard a Great Northern service to Potters Bar. Exit Potters Bar Station and from Stop B board the No. 398 Sullivan Buses service (to Watford Town Centre). Disembark at the undesignated stop (Motorway Service Station) on St Albans Road, turn left, walk 325 metres and this becomes Swanland Road. Continue along Swanland Road for 125 metres and after passing Lantern Services turn right into Wash Lane. Walk 780 metres to a curve in the road with a small lane branching off to the right and this is the location seen in the film with trees lining the left and right of the road.

Then

Now

Wash Lane in 2015, now closed to traffic, was once a much-used road into London but was to be replaced by the A1 which runs adjacent to it to the right of shot.

Location 126: The Hump-Backed Bridge

Film: *On the Buses*

Wash Lane, Potters Bar, Hertfordshire, EN6 3QQ.

Travelling at speed we see the motorbike and sidecar go over a hump-backed bridge, sending it airborne for an instant (exactly 69 minutes 57 into the film). This scene was filmed on Wash Lane near Potters Bar and the road is no longer open to public traffic. The road itself has fallen into disrepair but the bridge remains with a couple of trees still present, lining one side of the road. However, today, in the background of this location stands a Days Inn Hotel with the land to the west of the northern stretch of Wash Lane now having been heavily redeveloped with another hotel, a motorway service station and a bus depot now situated where it was largely covered by fields.

How to get there: The most direct route to this location is via train from London King's Cross Station aboard a Great Northern service to Potters Bar. Exit Potters Bar Station and from Stop B board the No. 398 Sullivan Buses service (to Watford Town Centre). Disembark at the undesignated stop (Motorway Service Station) on St Albans Road, turn left, walk 325 metres and this becomes Swanland Road. Continue along Swanland Road for 125 metres and after passing Lantern Services turn right into Wash Lane. Walk 610 metres, crossing the hump-backed bridge the motorbike and sidecar leapt over in the film, and turn to photograph from the direction the motorbike travelled.

Then

Now

The bridge's more arched wall seen in the film has today been replaced.

Location 127: The Sidecar Splits

Film: *On the Buses*

Rectory Lane, Shenley, Hertfordshire, WD7 9BX.

As the sidecar nears a junction on a country lane, the motorbike turns to head in one direction whilst the sidecar splits and heads in another direction (69 minutes 4 seconds into the film). Just ahead is a triangular traffic island covered in grass with a dishevelled-looking green wooden bench, a sign post, a telegraph pole and ornate lamp post all present on this traffic island. This scene was filmed on Rectory Lane at the junction of Harris Lane in the village of Shenley and today very little has changed. Aside from the lamp post being relocated slightly and changed in design and the bench now being concrete-based with a wooden seat, then the location is instantly recognisable.

How to get there: The most direct route to this location is via train from London St Pancras Station (Lower Level) aboard a Thameslink service to Elstree and Borehamwood Station. Exit Elstree and Borehamwood Station and from Stop B board the No. 658 Uno service (to St Albans). Disembark at the undesignated stop (Black Lion) on London Road, turn left and cross the road. Walk 420 metres along Rectory Lane until reaching the traffic island prominent in this scene.

Then

Now

The sidecar takes the left turn and the motorbike turns right.

Location 128: The Sidecar Comes to a Stop

Film: *On the Buses*

Mimms Lane, Shenley, Hertfordshire, WD7 9AP.

The runaway sidecar runs down a country lane before running into a grassy bank and fence which brings it to a halt (69 minutes 13 seconds into the film). In the background is a barn and behind that is a farm. This scene was filmed in Mimms Lane in Shenley and today the location has altered slightly. The grassy verge in which the sidecar runs onto remains, but the wooden fence seen in the film has been replaced by a six-foot high hedge. The barn in the background has changed in appearance with the brickwork seen in the film covered largely by wooden cladding and the small adjoining structure seen in the film has been demolished and replaced by a brick wall. Also noticeable is that the trees lining the road have grown a great deal in both size and number.

How to get there: The most direct route to this location is via train from London St Pancras Station (Lower Level) aboard a Thameslink service to Elstree and Borehamwood Station. Exit Elstree and Borehamwood Station and from Stop B board the No. 658 Uno service (to St Albans). Disembark at the undesignated stop (Black Lion) on London Road, turn left, cross the road and walk 420 metres along Rectory Lane until reaching the traffic island and take the right turn into Harris Lane. Walk for 45 metres and turn left into Mimms Lane, then walk 30 metres to a road sign warning for heavy goods vehicles on the right side of the road. Across the road is the grassy verge where the sidecar came to a halt.

Then

Now

The sidecar came to a rest where the blue road sign stands today.

Location 129: Stan Stops a Bus

Film: *On the Buses*

Mimms Lane, Shenley, Hertfordshire, WD7 9AP.

With Olive going into labour trapped in the sidecar, Stan runs out into a country lane to stop a passing bus (69 minutes 58 seconds into the film). In this scene the Rivendell Barn can be seen at the very edge of shot and on the other side of the lane is a grassy verge and sporadic trees with fields beyond them. This location, filmed in Mimms Lane in Shenley, today has seen the grassy verge diminish in size on the right of the lane and a greater number of trees grow there now. On the other side of the trees the fields have been replaced by a car park for an adjacent tree maintenance company.

How to get there: The most direct route to this location is via train from London St Pancras Station (Lower Level) aboard a Thameslink service to Elstree and Borehamwood Station. Exit Elstree and Borehamwood Station and from Stop B board the No. 658 Uno service (to St Albans). Disembark at the undesignated stop (Black Lion) on London Road, turn left, cross the road and walk 420 metres along Rectory Lane until reaching the traffic island and take the right turn into Harris Lane. Walk for 45 metres, turn left into Mimms Lane and walk 30 metres to a road sign warning for heavy goods vehicles on the left side of the road for a view down the lane where the bus is flagged down by Stan with the barn on the left.

Then

Now

Mimms Lane today has a more leafy appearance.

Location 130: Another Diversion

Film: *On the Buses*

Rowley Lane, Barnet, Hertfordshire, EN5 3HW.

A bus travels over a bridge spanning a motorway on its way to an unexpected meeting with another diversion sign (70 minutes 41 seconds into the film). On either side of the road is a small white fence with grassy verges beyond that. This scene was filmed on Rowley Lane as it crosses the A1 at the Barnet By-Pass section. Today the small fence remains but has lost its white paintwork and the grassy verge on the left side of the road has been replaced by a mixture of bushes and small trees. This location would have been shot from the pavement on the corner of the entrance into Rowley Lane on the east side of the A1.

How to get there: The most direct route to this location is via train from London King's Cross Station aboard a Great Northern service to Potters Bar. Exit Potters Bar Station and from Stop B board the No. 398 Sullivan Buses service (to Watford Town Centre). Disembark at the undesignated stop (Rowley Lane) and turn right and cross here. Turn left, walk 225 metres and cross Newark Green, then turn left to continue along Rowley Lane. Walk 250 metres across the bridge over the A1 on Rowley Lane until reaching the far pavement on the Rowley Lane entrance on the east side of the A1 where this scene would have been filmed.

Then

Now

The road layout is unchanged in 2016 aside from the island placed at the turn into Rowley Lane.

Location 131: Diverting onto a Motorway

Film: *On the Buses*

Rowley Lane, Barnet, Hertfordshire, EN5 3HW.

A false diversion sign is seen by the roadside as a bus approaches it (70 minutes 44 seconds into the film). The bus follows the sign though and, moments later, takes a tight left-hand turn passing the sign and heading onto a motorway. In the background a wooden fence follows the road around and fields can be seen beyond. The sign was located on the east side of the A1 at the Barnet By-Pass section of the motorway on the exit out of Rowley Lane leading onto the A1. Today the location beyond the sign has changed a little. Whereas in the film Stan and Jack emerge from a dip in the terrain to remove the sign, today that area is now somewhat overgrown with bushes and is inaccessible on the eastern side of Rowley Lane at the entrance onto the southbound entrance to the A1. On the corner of Rowley Lane where the diversion sign stood is a low emission traffic signpost.

How to get there: The most direct route to this location is via train from London King's Cross Station aboard a Great Northern service to Potters Bar. Exit Potters Bar Station and from Stop B board the No. 398 Sullivan Buses service (to Watford Town Centre). Disembark at the undesignated stop (Rowley Lane) and turn right and cross here. Turn left, walk 225 metres and cross Newark Green, then turn left to continue along Rowley Lane. Walk 245 metres across the bridge over the A1 on Rowley Lane until reaching the near pavement on the Rowley Lane entrance on the east side of the A1. Across the road is now a low emission traffic signpost by the road where the diversion is seen in the film.

Then

Now

The diversion sign stood where the light grey patch can be seen on the pavement directly ahead.

Location 132: St Luke's Maternity Hospital

Film: *On the Buses*

Shenley Road, Borehamwood, Hertfordshire, WD6 1EQ.

After giving birth to her first son, Arthur, Olive exits St Luke's Maternity Hospital with the family (74 minutes 38 seconds into the film). Of course St Luke's was a fictional hospital and was merely an administration block at the far west of Elstree Studios on Shenley Road which was demolished in the early 1990s. Directly next to it a hotel can be seen. Today that hotel remains and is now the Elstree Inn, but where the fictional St Luke's hospital stood is now covered in trees and bushes and is the surrounding area of Tesco Extra's garage. Where Olive exits onto Shenley Road, there are a couple of public phone boxes there today.

How to get there: The most direct route to this location is via train from London St Pancras Station (Lower Level) aboard a Thameslink service to Elstree and Borehamwood Station. Exit Elstree and Borehamwood Station and from Stop A board the No. 107 bus (to New Barnet) or the No. 292 bus (to Colindale). Disembark at the undesignated stop (Borehamwood Tesco) which is three stops into your journey. Turn right and walk 20 metres to the level crossing to cross here. Turn right again and walk 80 metres, turning sharp left onto Shenley Road. On your left are the public phone boxes marking the spot where Olive exited the hospital.

Then

Now

Bushes now stand where an administration block – part of the demolished portion of Elstree Studios which doubled as St Luke's Maternity Hospital.

Location 133: Sally's House

Film: *On the Buses*

Bullhead Road, Borehamwood, Hertfordshire, WD6 1RJ.

In an attempt to rekindle his romance with Sally, Stan visits her house on a dark evening (78 minutes 10 seconds into the film). The red-bricked semi-detached house sits in a long line of houses with a garden hedge and French windows. This was No. 188 Bullhead Road in Borehamwood and today the property has changed very little, with the windows and door seemingly identical although a garden hedge is only present on one side of the garden now. Incidentally, I would very confidently say that the window on the right side of the property that Stan is seen knocking on was filmed at the studios and not at No. 188, as the front door on this property suggests a hall and not a bedroom as we see in the film.

How to get there: The most direct route to this location is via train from London St Pancras Station (Lower Level) aboard a Thameslink service to Elstree and Borehamwood Station. Exit Elstree and Borehamwood Station and from Stop B board the No. 306 Sullivan Buses service (to Watford) and disembark at the undesignated stop (Thornbury Gardens). Turn left and walk 20 metres along Arundel Drive before turning right into Thornbury Gardens. Walk 90 metres and turn left to cross at the entrance to your left into Bullhead Road. Walk 180 metres to No. 188 Bullhead Road on your left – Sally's house in the film.

Then

Now

Sally's house which Stan visits at dusk.

Location 134: The Closing Credits

Film: *On the Buses*

Brook Road, Borehamwood, Hertfordshire, WD6 5EQ.

The closing credits begin to roll as a bus is seen travelling down a road lined by a park with trees in it on one side of the road and housing on the other side of the road, with the photograph below seen at 83 minutes 12 seconds into the film. This sequence was filmed on Brook Road with Aberford Park on the left with the bus heading southwards into the town centre and is first seen having passed the Gateshead Road junction and follows the bus to when it has just passed Borehamwood FC's ground to the far right, approaching the end of Brook Road. The stretch of road remains much the same aside from a greater number of trees in the park and some new properties built on the right.

How to get there: The most direct route to this location is via train from London St Pancras Station (Lower Level) aboard a Thameslink service to Elstree and Borehamwood Station. Exit Elstree and Borehamwood Station and from Stop A board the No. 306 Sullivan Buses service (to Borehamwood Tesco). Disembark at the undesignated stop (Warenford Way) on Brook Road, turn left and cross here to approximately where the bus passes, heading south in the closing credits.

Then

Now

Brook Road in 2015 which Stan's bus travels down in the closing credits.

Location 135: Buses Parked Back-to-Back

Film: *Mutiny on the Buses*

Brook Road, Borehamwood, Hertfordshire, WD6 5HG.

The camera pans in on two buses parked back-to-back next to a row of houses (as *Mutiny on the Buses* starts just 25 seconds into the film). These buses were parked at the side of No. 12 Brook Road in Borehamwood and the location today has changed very little, although the hedge running alongside the bus has now grown a great deal. The six-foot high wooden fence does remain and the property itself has undergone only minor changes such as windows having been double-glazed. This location was used identically at the end of the film as well and would have been filmed with a camera positioned on the top of Neptune House in what is now BBC Elstree Studios. It pans around from a large block of flats called Canterbury House before zooming in on two buses parked back-to-back on Brook Road. Curiously though, the exterior shots of this scene seconds later were filmed in a totally different location.

How to get there: The most direct route to this location is via train from London St Pancras Station (Lower Level) aboard a Thameslink service to Elstree and Borehamwood Station. Exit Elstree and Borehamwood Station and from Stop A board the No. 306 Sullivan Buses service (to Borehamwood Tesco). Disembark at the undesignated stop (St Teresa's School) on Brook Road, turn right and walk 130 metres until just past a small traffic island. Across the road is the house that Stan's bus is parked next to with another bus behind.

Then

Now

Two buses parked here in the opening scene of *Mutiny on the Buses* but seen from a much more elevated angle in the film.

Location 136: A Third Bus Arrives on the Scene

Film: *Mutiny on the Buses*

Brodewater Road, Borehamwood, Hertfordshire, WD6 5AJ.

With two buses parked back-to-back on a street lined by houses, another bus in the distance takes a right-hand turn into the street (1 minute 15 seconds into the film). The street has a pavement and grassy verge on either side of the road and the odd tree lines it as well. This scene was filmed on Brodewater Road in Borehamwood directly north of Borehamwood FC. The bus in the distance turns into the street out of Hartforde Road and today the street has barely changed. The tree seen in the film on the right side of the road has been removed whilst a tree on the other side of the road has grown somewhat, but most garden hedges do remain and houses have undergone only minor changes. The camera would have been positioned by the hedge to the right of No. 11 Brodewater Road looking north down the street to film this scene. At the end of this scene you can see the hedge and a path, as Blakey falls from the rear of Stan's bus, which is there at the end of Brodewater Road today. This helped to trace this location as did the creeping vine on the property seen in the film. This location appears again at the end of the film.

How to get there: The most direct route to this location is via train from London St Pancras Station (Lower Level) aboard a Thameslink service to Elstree and Borehamwood Station. Exit Elstree and Borehamwood Station and from Stop B board the No. 658 Uno service (to St Albans). Disembark at the undesignated stop (Aberford Road) on Brook Road, turn left, cross here and turn right to walk 60 metres along Brook Road. Turn left into Hartforde Road and walk 150 metres before turning right into Brodewater Road. Walk 70 metres and cross to the hedge to the right of No. 11 Brodewater Road to where the rear of Stan's bus was parked.

Then

Now

Brodewater Road in 2015 minus three buses.

Location 137: Theme Score Strikes Up

Film: *Mutiny on the Buses*

Shenley Road, Borehamwood, Hertfordshire, WD6 1AH.

As the opening score of *Mutiny on the Buses* starts we see Stan's bus drive down a main road with shops on either side with a church to the left in the background (2 minutes 38 seconds into the film). This scene was filmed on Shenley Road with the bus having just passed the entrance to Clarendon Road on the right. The church in the background is All Saints Church of England. A Woolworths store directly to the right of the bus is now an Iceland frozen foods store. Aside from the street having been narrowed, a brand new library being built on the left of the road and shops having changed owners, the street remains much the same. This section of Shenley Road is seen later in the opening credits as the motorbike and sidecar travels down it and Mum sees Stan and Susy entering a jeweller's shop.

How to get there: The most direct route to this location is via train from London St Pancras Station (Lower Level) aboard a Thameslink service to Elstree and Borehamwood Station. Exit Elstree and Borehamwood Station, turn left and walk for 55 metres before crossing Station Road and onto Shenley Road. Walk 375 metres eastwards along Shenley Road and roughly adjacent to the Nos. 135-141 Shenley Road (Iceland store) where Stan's bus is seen passing in this scene.

Then

Now

Seen in the opening credits of *Mutiny on the Buses*.

Location 138: Payne the Jeweller

Film: *Mutiny on the Buses*

Shenley Road, Borehamwood, Hertfordshire, WD6 1AH.

As the opening credits sequence of *Mutiny on the Buses* begin to roll, Susy is seen waving to Stan who has pulled up in his bus as she shops for her engagement ring at Payne – a jeweller's shop (2 minutes 49 seconds into the film). This jeweller's shop has ceased trading and is now a Betfred bookmakers at No. 159 Shenley Road in Borehamwood. The exterior of the shop has changed greatly with the centrally placed doors and angled window displays replaced by a door on the right of the shop with a flat window display today. Of course, Stan's bus would have been parked adjacent to the shop when the motorbike and sidecar crashes into it later in the opening credits.

How to get there: The most direct route to this location is via train from London St Pancras Station (Lower Level) aboard a Thameslink service to Elstree and Borehamwood Station. Exit Elstree and Borehamwood Station, left and walk for 55 metres before crossing Station Road and onto Shenley Road. Walk 400 metres eastwards along Shenley Road and roughly adjacent is No. 159 Shenley Road (BetFred's) which was Payne's shop where Susy buys her engagement ring.

Then

Now

Susy buys her engagement ring.

Location 139: Motorbike and Sidecar Travelling Downhill

Film: *Mutiny on the Buses*

Bullhead Road, Borehamwood, Hertfordshire, WD6 1HP.

The motorbike and sidecar with Arthur, Olive and Mum aboard travels around a slight bend and downhill on a street lined by semi-detached houses and trees (2 minutes 57 seconds into the film). The motorbike is seen passing what is now No. 73 Bullhead Road in Borehamwood but it is apparent that new properties have been built on this site today and all trees have been removed that can be seen in the film. However, the location is identifiable by the curve in the road and the side view of the property in the rear with two windows at the side of the house and the drainpipe arrangement, which are all present today at this location.

How to get there: The most direct route to this location is via train from London St Pancras Station (Lower Level) aboard a Thameslink service to Elstree and Borehamwood Station. Exit Elstree and Borehamwood Station and from Stop A board the No. 292 bus (to Colindale). Disembark at the undesignated stop (Durham Road) and cross Manor Way before turning left and walking 50 metres. Turn right onto an unnamed path and walk 130 metres onto Bullhead Road, crossing here. Turn right and walk 40 metres until adjacent to a path leading between properties where it is likely this scene was filmed from by the camera crew.

Then

Now

The motorbike and sidecar would have been where the manhole cover is in the middle of the road.

Location 140: A Close-Up of the Motorbike and Sidecar

Film: *Mutiny on the Buses*

Gateshead Road, Borehamwood, Hertfordshire, WD6 5DZ.

An instant later the film offers a close-up of the motorbike and sidecar travelling west along a clearly different street lined by houses with small, grassy banked verges along the roadside (2 minutes 58 seconds into the film). This was filmed on Gateshead Road with the motorbike seen passing where No. 241 Gateshead Road is on the left of shot. The location today is much the same aside from cosmetic changes to the properties here and newer design of lamp posts now in place. This location can be pinpointed by the telegraph poles still in their original locations to the present day. Moments later the camera zooms in on Mum introducing her in the credits as the bike continues to travel down Gateshead Road.

How to get there: The most direct route to this location is via train from London St Pancras Station (Lower Level) aboard a Thameslink service to Elstree and Borehamwood Station. Exit Elstree and Borehamwood Station and from Stop A board the No. 306 Sullivan Buses service (to Borehamwood Tesco). Disembark at the undesignated stop (Reston Path) on Gateshead Road, turn right, walk 50 metres and cross the road where you are adjacent to No. 241 Gateshead Road where the motorbike and sidecar is seen heading west.

Then

Now

**Today parked cars line the road unlike in 1972 when
Mutiny on the Buses was filmed here.**

Location 141: Introducing Arthur

Film: *Mutiny on the Buses*

Gateshead Road, Borehamwood, Hertfordshire, WD6 5LW.

As the opening credits introduce Arthur, the motorbike and sidecar he is aboard travels along a street lined by houses with grassy verges between the kerb and pavement and in the background the road curves with two trees lining the road (3 minutes 21 seconds into the film). This scene was filmed in Gateshead Road with the motorbike passing roughly where No. 251 Gateshead Road is today. The location is much the same today aside from cosmetic changes to the houses, newer lamp posts in place and trees having grown to mask that house in the background.

How to get there: The most direct route to this location is via train from London St Pancras Station (Lower Level) aboard a Thameslink service to Elstree and Borehamwood Station. Exit Elstree and Borehamwood Station and from Stop A board the No. 306 Sullivan Buses service (to Borehamwood Tesco). Disembark at the undesignated stop (Reston Path) on Gateshead Road, turn left and walk 20 metres along Gateshead Road until reaching the pavement outside No. 223 Gateshead Road where the motorbike passes as Arthur is introduced in the film.

Then

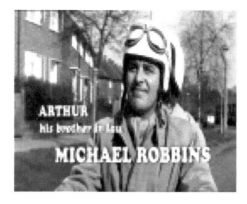

Now

The trees remain but have grown somewhat and solar panels can be seen on the roof of one property, obviously not present in 1972.

Location 142: Jack Collecting Fares

Film: *Mutiny on the Buses*

Manor Way, Borehamwood, Hertfordshire, WD6 2AA.

Stan's bus travels up an inclining street lined on one side by a row of shops, stops and Jack gets off and collects fares (3 minutes 59 seconds into the film). Over his shoulder, the end of the row of shops can be seen with two public telephone boxes against the wall and a road leading off in a westerly direction. This scene was filmed on Manor Way just past the junction of Arundel Drive with the bus parked on the south-westerly most point of Ripon Park. Today the location remains much the same although the public telephone boxes have been removed and the wall at the end of the Manor Way row of shops has a mural on it paying homage to the Muppet Show which was made in the town. The road that runs off in a westerly direction is Arundel Drive.

How to get there: The most direct route to this location is via train from London St Pancras Station (Lower Level) aboard a Thameslink service to Elstree and Borehamwood Station. Exit Elstree and Borehamwood Station and from Stop A board the No. 292 bus (to Colindale). Disembark at the undesignated stop (Ripon Park), turn left and walk 55 metres along Manor Way until reaching the junction with Arundel Drive where the rear of Stan's bus stopped.

Then

Now

**The view in the background as Jack collects fares as
the opening credits roll.**

Location 143: Jack Enters Ladbrokes

Film: *Mutiny on the Buses*

Watford Way, Edgware, London, NW7 3JR.

After collecting the bus fares he looks across the road (4 minutes 6 seconds into the film) to see a Ladbrokes bookmakers shop and walks across to it as the opening credits continue to roll. Although they made it appear that the Ladbrokes was at Manor Way in Borehamwood it was not – this particular Ladbrokes was located at No. 651 Watford Way in Edgware, London. Today that shop is now a beauty salon and is much different in appearance. Gone is the central doorway and angled windows with black surrounds and the windows now stretch down to ground level and run straight along the width of the shop to the door whilst the wooden door seen to the left of Ladbrokes has been boarded up.

How to get there: The most direct route to this location is via train from London St Pancras Station (Lower Level) aboard a Thameslink service to Mill Hill Broadway Station. Exit Mill Hill Broadway Station, turn left and walk 50 metres onto The Broadway, turning right to walk a further 40 metres to the level crossing. Cross here and turn right to walk 20 metres to Stop F (Mill Hill Broadway) and board the No. 186 bus (to Northwick Park Hospital). Disembark at Stop K (Apex Corner), turn right and cross Watford Way to the parade of shops. Turn right and walk 60 metres along Watford Way. On your right is No. 651 Watford Way which was formerly the Ladbrokes that Jack visits in the film.

Then

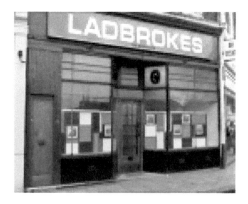

Now

Jack's bookmakers as it is today in 2016.

Location 144: Arthur's Driving Lessons

Film: *Mutiny on the Buses*

Rectory Lane, Shenley, Hertfordshire, WD7 9BX.

Stan gives Arthur instructions at this location (16 minutes 42 seconds into the film) before giving him lessons on how to drive a bus. The bus is parked in a lay-by next to a bus shelter with a large grassy expanse to the right and in the background a hedge, trees and in the distance a house. This location was used several times in *Mutiny on the Buses* such as further driving lesson scenes, Stan and Jack practising darts and when Blakey arrives in his new van. These scenes were filmed in Rectory Lane in the village of Shenley and today the location is virtually unchanged aside from a new property built across the road from the lay-by further down the lane. The lay-by remains but the bus shelter was clearly a temporary structure put in place for filming of the scene as there is no sign of the structure today.

How to get there: The most direct route to this location is via train from London St Pancras Station (Lower Level) aboard a Thameslink service to Elstree and Borehamwood Station. Exit Elstree and Borehamwood Station and from Stop B board the No. 658 Uno service (to St Albans). Disembark at the undesignated stop (Black Lion) on London Road, turn left and cross the road and walk 60 metres along Rectory Lane. Cross the road to arrive at the lay-by which Stan's bus often parked in.

Then

Now

This filming location was seen frequently in *Mutiny on the Buses*.

Location 145: Stan Hanging out of the Driver's Cab

Film: *Mutiny on the Buses*

Mimms Lane, Shenley, Hertfordshire, WD7 9AP.

Stan's bus runs out of control with Arthur in the driving seat (17 minutes 26 seconds into the film) and Stan hanging out of the door to the driver's cab as the bus turns a corner in a country lane. A house can be seen to the far right in the distance. To the left is the entrance to another country road and in the foreground is the side of a barn by the roadside. This scene was filmed with the bus travelling down Mimms Lane in Shenley with the entrance to Harris Lane on the left. The house seen in the distance is still present at the end of Rectory Lane but is now totally masked by trees and hedges, whilst the barn to the right of shot remains but has altered somewhat in appearance. We see this location from a different angle in the first spin-off film when the sidecar comes to rest on a grassy verge.

How to get there: The most direct route to this location is via train from London St Pancras Station (Lower Level) aboard a Thameslink service to Elstree and Borehamwood Station. Exit Elstree and Borehamwood Station and from Stop B board the No. 658 Uno service (to St Albans). Disembark at the undesignated stop (Black Lion) on London Road, turn left and cross the road and walk 420 metres along Rectory Lane until reaching the traffic island, then take the right turn into Harris Lane. Walk for 45 metres and turn left into Mimms Lane, then walk 40 metres to the side of the barn seen in the film on the left of the lane and turn around for the angle obtained by the camera looking back in the direction you have just travelled.

Then

Now

The country lane today has changed in appearance a great deal with a row of trees growing to the left and the barn on the right having undergone renovations.

Location 146: The Farmyard Crash

Film: *Mutiny on the Buses*

Chalk Hill Farm, Ridge, Hertfordshire, EN6 3LP.

A country farm is seen in its entirety (17 minutes 43 seconds into the film) moments before Stan's out of control bus swerves into the farmyard, depositing Stan in a pile of manure. This farm can be found in the village of Ridge on Deeves Hall Lane which is around three miles to the north-east of Borehamwood. The location today is still an active farm and remains very similar in structure aside from some slight refurbishments to the large barn on the right-hand side of the property, whilst a hedge now masks a large part of the wall on the left.

How to get there: The most direct route to this location is via train from London King's Cross Station aboard a Great Northern service to Potters Bar. Exit Potters Bar Station and from Stop B board the No. 398 Sullivan Buses service (to Watford Town Centre). Disembark at the undesignated stop (Clare Hall) and exit the car park area. At the junction, cross onto Crossoaks Lane and walk 525 metres before turning right into Deeves Hall Lane. Walk 10 metres to the gate of Church Farm seen in the film.

Then

Now

The farm Arthur crashes Stan's bus into as it looked in 2015.

Location 147: Motorbike and Sidecar Towed Uphill

Film: *Mutiny on the Buses*

Bullhead Road, Borehamwood, Hertfordshire, WD6 1HT.

Arthur and Olive are aboard the motorbike and sidecar minus its start lever as it is towed uphill by Stan's bus (23 minutes 40 seconds into the film). The road is lined by semi-detached houses and in the distance, at the bottom of the hill, is a college. This was filmed on Bullhead Road as the motorbike is just passing No. 56 Bullhead Road on the left. Today this location is much the same although new properties have replaced some houses on the right and the Oaklands College building seen in the film at the bottom of the road has been replaced by residential flats.

How to get there: The most direct route to this location is via train from London St Pancras Station (Lower Level) aboard a Thameslink service to Elstree and Borehamwood Station. Exit Elstree and Borehamwood Station and from Stop A board the No. 292 bus (to Colindale). Disembark at the undesignated stop (Durham Road) and cross Manor Way before turning left and walking 50 metres. Turn right onto an unnamed path and walk 130 metres onto Bullhead Road, crossing here. Turn right and walk 110 metres until at the pavement outside No. 52 Bullhead Road where the motorbike and sidecar is seen passing in the film.

Then

Now

The motorbike and sidecar was towed here but in 1972 the road was not so cluttered with parked cars.

Location 148: Towing Continues

Film: *Mutiny on the Buses*

Bullhead Road, Borehamwood, Hertfordshire, WD6 1HW.

The camera switches to a long-range angle picking up Stan's bus as it continues to tow the motorbike and sidecar (23 minutes 41 seconds into the film) along a flatter section of a street lined with houses. This shot was filmed at the bottom of the hill on Bullhead Road with the bus passing No. 12 Bullhead Road with the camera positioned on the pavement outside No. 23 Bullhead Road to film this part of the scene. Today, the only change to this location is that many of the properties on the right side of the road have had garden walls and hedges removed to allow their gardens to be used for parking their vehicles. Also, Oaklands College seen in the film has been replaced by residential flats.

How to get there: The most direct route to this location is via train from London St Pancras Station (Lower Level) aboard a Thameslink service to Elstree and Borehamwood Station. Exit Elstree and Borehamwood Station and from Stop A board the No. 107 (to New Barnet Station). Disembark at the undesignated stop (Studio Way) and turn left on Elstree Way and walk 200 metres before turning left to cross Elstree Way and onto Bullhead Road. Walk 150 metres until adjacent with No. 23 Bullhead Road where the camera was positioned to film this part of the scene.

Then

Now

**Stan's bus approaches the telegraph pole towing
Arthur's motorbike.**

Location 149: Towed to the Top of the Hill

Film: *Mutiny on the Buses*

Bullhead Road, Borehamwood, Hertfordshire, WD6 1HT.

With the motorbike and sidecar still being towed it reaches the top of a road on a sharp incline lined by houses (23 minutes 54 seconds into the film). As the camera picks them up the motorbike and sidecar are passing No. 80 Bullhead Road on its left with a telegraph pole just behind them and it follows the vehicle until passing No. 100 Bullhead Road when Arthur complains of the steering going stiff. The stretch of the road has had some properties being completely demolished and rebuilt since the film was shot here but topographically the road remains the same.

How to get there: The most direct route to this location is via train from London St Pancras Station (Lower Level) aboard a Thameslink service to Elstree and Borehamwood Station. Exit Elstree and Borehamwood Station and from Stop A board the No. 292 bus (to Colindale). Disembark at the undesignated stop (Durham Road) and cross Manor Way before turning left and walking 50 metres. Turn right onto an unnamed path and walk 130 metres onto Bullhead Road, crossing here. Turn right and walk 42 metres until at the pavement outside No. 80 Bullhead Road where the motorbike and sidecar is first seen passing in this part of the scene.

Then

Now

Trees are now more evident in 2015 on this section of Bullhead Road.

Location 150: Approaching a Traffic Island

Film: *Mutiny on the Buses*

Bullhead Road, Borehamwood, Hertfordshire, WD6 1HR.

After knocking a man painting lines on the road into his bucket of paint, moments later the bus continues to tow the motorbike and sidecar towards a traffic island covered in grass (24 minutes 28 seconds into the film). The bus is passing what is now No. 111 Bullhead Road on the right of the bus whilst the man covered in paint is in the distance in the middle of the road with No. 94 Bullhead Road to his left. Today a lot of the properties on either side of the road have been newly-built but the tree on the edge of the pavement outside No. 111 remains. The traffic island has been elongated somewhat but remains covered in grass and is still located at the entrance to Hillside Avenue, stretching back to the entrance to Kenilworth Drive on the other side of Bullhead Road. Also, the traffic island is now a crossing point – not the case when this scene was filmed here.

How to get there: The most direct route to this location is via train from London St Pancras Station (Lower Level) aboard a Thameslink service to Elstree and Borehamwood Station. Exit Elstree and Borehamwood Station and from Stop A board the No. 292 bus (to Colindale). Disembark at the undesignated stop (Kenilworth House) on Manor Way and cross here. Walk 60 metres to the roundabout, turn left onto Kenilworth Drive and walk 130 metres before turning right onto Bullhead Road and crossing onto the traffic island that is seen in the film.

Then

Now

The tree seen in the film remains on the right and the lamp post on the left is still there but is of a more modern design.

Location 151: Brace for Impact

Film: *Mutiny on the Buses*

Bullhead Road, Borehamwood, Hertfordshire, WD6 1HP.

As the traffic island cannot be avoided, Arthur braces for impact leaning back on the motorbike and grimacing (24 minutes 31 seconds into the film). The motorbike is on a downhill slope and in the road just behind them are two manhole covers (key to pinpointing this location). Behind them, small trees grow on either side of the road at the top of the hill and a large garden hedge is prominent at the property over Arthur's right shoulder. This brief shot was of the motorbike and sidecar heading north passing No. 49 Bullhead Road on the left as we look at it.

How to get there: The most direct route to this location is via train from London St Pancras Station (Lower Level) aboard a Thameslink service to Elstree and Borehamwood Station. Exit Elstree and Borehamwood Station and from Stop A board the No. 292 bus (to Colindale). Disembark at the undesignated stop (Durham Road) and cross Manor Way before turning left and walking 50 metres. Turn right onto an unnamed path and walk 130 metres onto Bullhead Road. Turn right again and walk 120 metres to the pavement outside No. 49 Bullhead Road where Arthur braces for impact.

Then

Now

The large garden hedge remains to the left as do the two manhole covers in the road.

Location 152: Bus Pulls into a Side Street

Film: *Mutiny on the Buses*

Kenilworth Drive, Borehamwood, Hertfordshire, WD6 1QD.

When the motorbike's handlebars snap off it leads to Jack ringing the bell for the bus to stop which pulls into a side street (24 minutes 38 seconds into the film). The side street is lined by houses with grass verges on the pavements and trees on either side of the road. The bus was filmed turning left out of Bullhead Road into Kenilworth Drive although the property on the corner (now No. 115 Bullhead Road) has been newly-built, replacing the property that stood there for filming. The clue to this location is the tree by the side of the road and grassy verge which are all still present to the current day. However, the tree seen on the very right of shot is no longer there.

How to get there: The most direct route to this location is via train from London St Pancras Station (Lower Level) aboard a Thameslink service to Elstree and Borehamwood Station. Exit Elstree and Borehamwood Station and from Stop A board the No. 292 bus (to Colindale). Disembark at the undesignated stop (Kenilworth House) on Manor Way and cross here. Walk 60 metres to the roundabout, turn left onto Kenilworth Drive and walk 130 metres before crossing Bullhead Road to reach the position at which this scene would have probably been filmed.

Then

Now

Stan's bus pulled to a stop where the two cars are parked.

Location 153: The Workman's Tent

Film: *Mutiny on the Buses*

Bullhead Road, Borehamwood, Hertfordshire, WD6 1HS.

With the motorbike and sidecar running out of control downhill without its handlebars a workman's tent sits in the middle of the road ahead (24 minutes 49 seconds into the film). With houses on either side of the road the tent was positioned adjacent to No. 40 Bullhead Road. This can be accurately pinpointed as that property on the left of shot today still has the same garden wall and the telegraph pole and lamp post (though newer in design) are still present as well in the background. Also, on the right the bungalows offer another clue and remain there today.

How to get there: The most direct route to this location is via train from London St Pancras Station (Lower Level) aboard a Thameslink service to Elstree and Borehamwood Station. Exit Elstree and Borehamwood Station and from Stop A board the No. 292 bus (to Colindale). Disembark at the undesignated stop (Durham Road) and cross Manor Way before turning left and walking 50 metres. Turn right onto an unnamed path and walk 130 metres onto Bullhead Road. Cross Bullhead Road, turn right and walk 190 metres to the pavement outside No. 40 Bullhead Road where the workman's tent was positioned adjacent in the middle of the road.

Then

Now

The workman's tent stood to the right of the car in the centre of shot.

Location 154: Olive Stuck in a Manhole

Film: *Mutiny on the Buses*

Bullhead Road, Borehamwood, Hertfordshire, WD6 1HS.

After the motorbike and sidecar had ran into the workman's tent and running onwards, Olive is left behind stuck in a manhole in the middle of the road (24 minutes 55 seconds into the film). This manhole was located directly adjacent to No. 32 Bullhead Road and remains there to this day. The clues to this location are the telegraph pole and lamp post present in the background in the film and still there today. However, some of the roadside properties have been rebuilt whilst others have knocked down garden walls to enable them to park their cars in what was the garden area. This manhole features later in the film when Stan's dartboard falls from the bus and rolls into the open manhole.

How to get there: The most direct route to this location is via train from London St Pancras Station (Lower Level) aboard a Thameslink service to Elstree and Borehamwood Station. Exit Elstree and Borehamwood Station and from Stop A board the No. 292 bus (to Colindale). Disembark at the undesignated stop (Durham Road) and cross Manor Way before turning left and walking 50 metres. Turn right onto an unnamed path and walk 130 metres onto Bullhead Road. Cross Bullhead Road, turn right and walk 200 metres to the pavement outside No. 32 Bullhead Road and in the middle of the road is the manhole which Olive was stuck in.

Then

Now

**The manhole cover Olive gets stuck in with parked cars
now encroaching on it.**

Location 155: Arthur Rescued

Film: *Mutiny on the Buses*

Bullhead Road, Borehamwood, Hertfordshire, WD6 1HS.

Arthur, who had collected the workman's tent and workman aboard his runaway motorbike and sidecar, crashes into a telegraph pole and is rescued by Stan and Jack who pull the workman's tent off (25 minutes 11 seconds into the film). This telegraph pole was and still is situated on the pavement between No. 22 and No. 24 Bullhead Road and this can be ascertained by the unusual garden wall in shot, with three distinct patterns along the middle of the structure, which is still present at No. 22 today. Also note the arched doorways in the background which can also been seen in the film.

How to get there: The most direct route to this location is via train from London St Pancras Station (Lower Level) aboard a Thameslink service to Elstree and Borehamwood Station. Exit Elstree and Borehamwood Station and from Stop A board the No. 107 (to New Barnet Station). Disembark at the undesignated stop (Studio Way), turn left on Elstree Way and walk 200 metres before turning left to cross Elstree Way and onto Bullhead Road. Walk 125 metres until adjacent with Nos. 22 and 24 Bullhead Road where the telegraph pole that the motorbike and sidecar crashes into in the film.

Then

Now

Arthur's motorbike crashed into this telegraph pole.

Location 156: Policemen in Patrol Car Contacted by Mistake

Film: *Mutiny on the Buses*

Torworth Road, Borehamwood, Hertfordshire, WD6 4EY.

Inspector Blake contacts a police car instead of one of his buses after the radio control system has been tampered with by Jack (28 minutes 26 seconds into the film). The police car is seen parked in a back street with the rear of a four-storey block of flats prominent in the background. This scene was filmed on Torworth Road and the four-storey structure in the background is the rear of the row of shops and flats above them on Leeming Road and Aycliffe Road. Today the location is almost identical aside from a black metal gate now in place where in the film there is a gap leading into the backyard of the properties in the background and the wall configuration has altered over the years.

How to get there: The most direct route to this location is via train from London St Pancras Station (Lower Level) aboard a Thameslink service to Elstree and Borehamwood Station. Exit Elstree and Borehamwood Station and from Stop C board the No. 292 bus (to Rossington Avenue). Disembark at the undesignated stop (Baldock Way), turn left to walk 140 metres along Aycliffe Road and turn right into Torworth Road, then walk 55 metres until adjacent to a six-foot high wall which the police car is seen being parked alongside on the other side of the road in the film.

Then

Now

The police car was parked adjacent to the wall in the foreground on the right.

Location 157: Policeman on his Beat Contacted by Mistake

Film: *Mutiny on the Buses*

Manor Way, Borehamwood, Hertfordshire, WD6 1QX.

As Inspector Blake tries once again to reach Stan on the radio control system he instead contacts a policeman on his walkie-talkie as he walks past a row of shops (29 minutes 15 seconds into the film). This scene was filmed at the southern end of Manor Way's parade of shops and the policeman is passing what is now No. 148 Manor Way and is a chemist shop today as it looks like it was in the film as well. The exact location can be pinpointed by the tiling at the foot of the chemist today which is present in the film. Also, the black railings above the shop run at different levels above the shops, which was a clue, as was the very broad boarding above the Clark's shoe shop in the film which is now an Indian takeaway and still has the broad boarding above it.

How to get there: The most direct route to this location is via train from London St Pancras Station (Lower Level) aboard a Thameslink service to Elstree and Borehamwood Station. Exit Elstree and Borehamwood Station and from Stop A board the No. 292 bus (to Colindale). Disembark at the undesignated stop (Ripon Park), turn left and walk 55 metres along Manor Way until reaching the junction with Arundel Drive. Turn left and cross Manor Way, then turn right and cross Arundel Drive. Walk 10 metres and on your left is the chemist which the policeman passes in the film as Inspector Blake contacts him by mistake.

Then

Now

**The parade of shops the policeman walks past as he is
contacted by Blakey.**

Location 158: The Gasworks

Film: *Mutiny on the Buses*

Station Road, Borehamwood, Hertfordshire, WD6 1GR.

The policemen in their patrol car, earlier ordered to the gasworks by Inspector Blake, are seen arriving at their destination (30 minutes 27 seconds into the film). In the background are two large, grey gas cylinders at the end of a road which is lined by small industrial-type structures on the right and what looks like an office block on the left. This scene was filmed in Station Road that runs adjacent to Elstree and Borehamwood's railway station. Today the view is very different, with the amalgamation of wooden huts and industrial buildings replaced on the right by residential flats and a car park, and to the left the office block has gone and been replaced by more residential flats. The gas cylinders do remain but are now painted a leaf green colour.

How to get there: The most direct route to this location is via train from London St Pancras Station (Lower Level) aboard a Thameslink service to Elstree and Borehamwood Station. Exit Elstree and Borehamwood Station, turn right and walk 60 metres onto Station Road at the far right of the station's car park. Turn right and walk 5 metres to the telegraph pole and ahead are the gasworks and the road the police car speeds down.

Then

Now

The gasworks today minus the police car.

Location 159: The Estate Agent

Film: *Mutiny on the Buses*

Aycliffe Road, Borehamwood, Hertfordshire, WD6 4EG.

Stan and Susy exit an estate agents, failing in their hunt for a flat with the disenchanted Susy walking off in a huff (37 minutes 53 seconds into the film). To Stan's left is the estate agent and he runs to catch an approaching bus. This scene was filmed on Aycliffe Road with the estate agents now being Johnny's Plaice – a fish bar at No. 170 Aycliffe Road. The location today has changed somewhat, with the grassy verge outside what was the estate agent replaced by raised flower beds and benches, whilst trees on the opposite side of the road have increased in size and number.

How to get there: The most direct route to this location is via train from London St Pancras Station (Lower Level) aboard a Thameslink service to Elstree and Borehamwood Station. Exit Elstree and Borehamwood Station and from Stop C board the No. 292 bus (to Rossington Avenue). Disembark at the undesignated stop (Baldock Way), turn left to walk 135 metres along Aycliffe Road and on your right is Johnny's Plaice which was the estate agent shop in the film.

Then

Now

The estate agent in the film seen in 2015 with orange shutters.

Location 160: Dustbins Knocked Over

Film: *Mutiny on the Buses*

Clarendon Road, Borehamwood, Hertfordshire, WD6 1BE.

Olive boards the motorbike and sidecar and heads to the bus depot to check up on Arthur (56 minutes 22 seconds into the film) and she crashes into a line of dustbins placed on the pavement edge, scattering rubbish everywhere. The dustbins she is seen about to hit were placed outside No. 53 Clarendon Road in Borehamwood and today the noticeable difference is the road is now lined by a great deal more parked traffic than was the case in the early 1970s, although the houses on either side of the road remain much the same.

How to get there: The most direct route to this location is via train from London St Pancras Station (Lower Level) aboard a Thameslink service to Elstree and Borehamwood Station. Exit Elstree and Borehamwood Station, turn left and walk for 55 metres before crossing Station Road and onto Shenley Road. Cross Shenley Road and walk 290 metres eastwards along Shenley Road before turning left into Clarendon Road and cross here. Walk 190 metres and on your right is No. 53 Clarendon Road and the pavement outside is where the dustbins were placed.

Then

Now

Clarendon Road without the metal dustbins in 2015.

Location 161: Crossing the Traffic Island

Film: *Mutiny on the Buses*

Bullhead Road, Borehamwood, Hertfordshire, WD6 1RQ.

As Olive continues her reckless journey to the bus depot aboard the motorbike and sidecar she mounts a grass-covered traffic island in a road lined by semi-detached houses (58 minutes 59 seconds into the film). This was filmed on Bullhead Road with the camera positioned roughly on the pavement outside No. 177 Bullhead Road looking north with the motorbike travelling south towards the camera. Today the houses on either side of the road remain much the same aside from garden hedges being removed from some properties, whilst the traffic island still has the traffic cones on it along with the grass covering but a tree now grows on it centrally, unlike in the film.

How to get there: The most direct route to this location is via train from London St Pancras Station (Lower Level) aboard a Thameslink service to Elstree and Borehamwood Station. Exit Elstree and Borehamwood Station and from Stop B board the No. 306 Sullivan Buses service (to Watford) and disembark at the undesignated stop (Thornbury Gardens). Turn left and walk 20 metres along Arundel Drive before turning right into Thornbury Gardens. Walk 90 metres and turn left to cross at the entrance to your left into Bullhead Road. Walk 200 metres and cross the road to reach the pavement, with No. 177 Bullhead Road on your right where this scene was filmed.

Then

Now

Olive takes the motorbike and sidecar across this traffic island.

Location 162: Approaching Windsor Safari Park

Film: *Mutiny on the Buses*

Winkfield Road, Windsor, Berkshire, SL4 4AY.

The depot's new tour bus approaches Windsor Safari Park as it travels along a dual carriageway (68 minutes 31 seconds into the film). This scene was filmed on Winkfield Road (also known as the B3022) a few metres to the south of the entrance into Windsor Safari Park. Of course, today Windsor Safari Park has become Legoland and the whole site has changed beyond recognition. Today, the road which the tour bus is seen travelling along has more trees growing on either side of the road and the road configuration has changed.

How to get there: The most direct route to this location is via train from Paddington Station aboard a First Great Western service to Slough Station. Exit Slough Station and walk 20 metres onto Brunel Way, turning right and walking 75 metres before turning left into Slough Bus Station. From Stop 10 board the No. 702 First Bus service (to Bracknell Bus Station) and disembark at the undesignated stop (Legoland Staff Entrance). Turn right and walk 10 metres, turn right and cross here and continue to walk 60 metres onto Winkfield Road. With the roundabout on your left, cross at the traffic island onto the far side of the road and to your right on the opposite side of the road is the stretch of road the tour bus travels along in the film.

Then

Now

The tour bus is seen travelling along this road – the silver birch tree near the lamp post can be seen in the film.

Location 163: Entrance to Windsor Safari Park

Film: *Mutiny on the Buses*

Winkfield Road, Windsor, Berkshire, SL4 4AY.

The tour bus is seen arriving at the entrance gates to Windsor Safari Park (68 minutes 42 seconds into the film). The gate huts where tickets/payments were collected are seen in the shot as are three distinctive roads leading into and out of the park with grassy verges in between. Today though it has all changed with the gate huts having long since been removed when Legoland took over the park and, where these gates stood, today is a road leading into the park for park and ride traffic, marked by two blue road signs on either side of the road. Also, if you look closely, when the bus exits the park at speed later in the film there is a very old looking tree to the far right of shot and, look behind bushes behind the large yellow Lego bricks to the right of centre of the shot today and you can still see that old tree.

How to get there: The most direct route to this location is via train from Paddington Station aboard a First Great Western service to Slough Station. Exit Slough Station and walk 20 metres onto Brunel Way turning right and walking 75 metres before turning left into Slough Bus Station. From Stop 10 board the No. 702 First Bus service (to Bracknell Bus Station) and disembark at the undesignated stop (Legoland Staff Entrance). Turn right and walk 10 metres, turn right to cross here and, reaching the pavement turnaround, see the blue road signs where the gate huts to Windsor Safari Park roughly stood.

Then

Now

The entrance to what was Windsor Safari Park as it looked in 2015.

Location 164: The Main Building at Pontins Prestatyn Sands Camp

Film: *Holiday on the Buses*

Barkby Avenue, Prestatyn, Denbighshire, LL19 7LA.

Stan and Jack are about to be introduced to their new boss and later their bus at the main building's entrance at the holiday camp (6 minutes 12 seconds into *Holiday on the Buses*). The main building seen in the film remains in the same place today but with slight refurbishments as an extension to the front of the building is now in place. Also, the brickwork façade has been replaced by a bright blue façade and entry into the building is on the same level, unlike in the film where there were steps up into the main building. This location is seen from various angles throughout the film.

How to get there: The most direct route to this location from Prestatyn Station is to exit the station at the Sandy Lane exit via the staircase. Walk 10 metres, turn right onto Station Road and walk for 150 metres before turning right onto Marine Road. After 500 metres cross the road and turn onto Marine Road East before turning sharply left onto Barkby Avenue. After 200 metres turn left and walk 70 metres to the gates to the holiday camp where, to gain access to the camp, an entrance fee will apply. On entering the camp, walk 180 metres to the main building's entrance on your right as seen in the film.

Then

This shot would have been taken from an elevated hoist positioned in the south-east corner of the holiday camp.

Now

The revamped main building from ground level at Pontins Prestatyn Sands.

Location 165: Main Gates at Pontins Prestatyn Sands Camp

Film: *Holiday on the Buses*

Barkby Avenue, Prestatyn, Denbighshire, LL19 7LA.

Stan and Jack are on their first trip aboard the holiday camp bus and it approaches the gates of the holiday camp (8 minutes 9 seconds into the film). The lavish grey gates have a blue letter P adorned on each gate and stone pillars with ornate lamps on top of those with the holiday camp's swimming pool visible in the background. Today, the gates are now black in colour and the letter P remains on each gate but are now a lighter blue in colour and there is now a pole across the entrance (unseen in the photograph) that moves up and is now operated by the security staff to allow traffic access to the camp. On the pillar on the left a plaque is now in place paying homage to *Holiday on the Buses* which was filmed there. The swimming pool is still visible in the background as well. These gates are to be seen later in the film as the family arrive at the camp.

How to get there: The most direct route to this location from Prestatyn Station is to exit the station at the Sandy Lane exit via the staircase. Walk 10 metres, turn right onto Station Road and walk for 150 metres before turning right onto Marine Road. After 500 metres cross the road and turn onto Marine Road East before turning sharply left onto Barkby Avenue. After 200 metres turn left and walk 70 metres to the gates to the holiday camp that feature in this scene.

Then

Now

The holiday camp gates remain identical in 2015 but are now painted black.

Location 166: Stan Meets Blakey

Film: *Holiday on the Buses*

Barkby Avenue, Prestatyn, Denbighshire, LL19 7LA.

After Stan's bus is forced to stop at the closed camp gates and he calls for them to be opened, Blakey exits the security office by the gates giving both a nasty shock (8 minutes 18 seconds into the film). The light brown-bricked building has a maroon-coloured door with the word SECURITY on it on a blue board and white lettering. Today the building remains virtually unchanged and is where security staff are based. The door is now painted blue with the lettering having been removed.

How to get there: The most direct route to this location from Prestatyn Station is to exit the station at the Sandy Lane exit via the staircase. Walk 10 metres, turn right onto Station Road and walk for 150 metres before turning right onto Marine Road. After 500 metres cross the road and turn onto Marine Road East before turning sharply left onto Barkby Avenue. After 200 metres turn left and walk 70 metres to the gates to the holiday camp and the security office is on the left as you pass through the gates.

Then

Now

The security office where Blakey once lurked.

Location 167: Inspecting the Staff

Film: *Holiday on the Buses*

Barkby Avenue, Prestatyn, Denbighshire, LL19 7LA.

The Chief Security Inspector Blake inspects his staff (10 minutes 34 seconds into the film) outside the main building. In the background the west side of the swimming pool building can be seen and today the building remains identical aside from slight refurbishment and the doors having been repainted – changing from yellow (in the film) to blue nowadays, but the grass verges all remain as does the road that runs through the camp in the background. Also, parked traffic today is much more in evidence today than was the case in 1973.

How to get there: The most direct route to this location from Prestatyn Station is to exit the station at the Sandy Lane exit via the staircase. Walk 10 metres, turn right onto Station Road and walk for 150 metres before turning right onto Marine Road. After 500 metres cross the road and turn onto Marine Road East before turning sharply left onto Barkby Avenue. After 200 metres turn left and walk 70 metres to the gates to the holiday camp where, to gain access to the camp, an entrance fee will apply. On entering the camp, walk 170 metres to the right of the main building's entrance and look to the west side of the swimming pool building as seen in the film.

Then

Now

Blakey inspects his staff where the cars are parked today, with the side of the swimming pool seen in the background.

Location 168: Meet the Camp Nurse

Film: *Holiday on the Buses*

Barkby Avenue, Prestatyn, Denbighshire, LL19 7LA.

Joan, the camp nurse, exits the first aid room to greet Inspector Blake as he walks by with Stan and Jack (11 minutes 16 seconds into the film). The first aid room's door was painted a khaki green colour with a Red Cross sign on it and was situated at the end of a single-storey block and had a small path outside it lined by a small wooden fence. Today this single-storey block remains but the door is painted blue with the red cross sign removed and the small wooden fence lining the path is no longer present, whilst the small tree obviously recently planted seen over Stan's shoulder in the film has been removed today. The exterior of the first aid room features again later in the film.

How to get there: The most direct route to this location from Prestatyn Station is to exit the station at the Sandy Lane exit via the staircase. Walk 10 metres, turn right onto Station Road and walk for 150 metres before turning right onto Marine Road. After 500 metres cross the road and turn onto Marine Road East before turning sharply left onto Barkby Avenue. After 200 metres turn left and walk 70 metres to the gates to the holiday camp where, to gain access to the camp, an entrance fee will apply. On entering the camp, walk 100 metres and to your right is the single-storey block and the door to the far left was the entrance to the first aid room in the film.

Then

Now

The first aid room now used as a storage room for the camp's tricycles.

Location 169: Mavis and her Mum aboard a Tricycle

Film: *Holiday on the Buses*

Barkby Avenue, Prestatyn, Denbighshire, LL19 7LA.

The holidaymaker Mavis and her bossy mum ride through the holiday camp on one of the camp's tricycles (14 minutes 14 seconds into the film). To the left of shot can be seen the top of the swimming pool building and in the distance through the crowds down the road the security office by the gates can just be seen and on the right of shot is a car park. This scene was filmed on the entrance road that comes in through the gates and runs passed the main building of the camp. In this scene the tricycle was heading west just having passed the swimming pool. Today this location remains much the same.

How to get there: The most direct route to this location from Prestatyn Station is to exit the station at the Sandy Lane exit via the staircase. Walk 10 metres, turn right onto Station Road and walk for 150 metres before turning right onto Marine Road. After 500 metres cross the road and turn onto Marine Road East before turning sharply left onto Barkby Avenue. After 200 metres turn left and walk 70 metres to the gates to the holiday camp where, to gain access to the camp, an entrance fee will apply. On entering the camp, walk 165 metres to the right of the main building's entrance and looking east up towards the camp gates is where the tricycle passes the swimming pool building in the film.

Then

Now

The stretch of road which Mavis and her mum cycle down.

Location 170: Broken Down Motorbike and Sidecar

Film: *Holiday on the Buses*

Barnet Lane, Borehamwood, Hertfordshire, WD6 3JF.

Arthur sits aboard the motorbike and sidecar as it is pushed by Olive, Mum and little Arthur up an inclining road with a long line of traffic behind it (14 minutes 48 seconds into the film). The road is lined by trees on either side and is on a sharp bend with lamp posts and sharp right road signs on the left side of the road. This scene was filmed on Barnet Lane in Borehamwood at the junction of Deacons Hill Road, with the motorbike being pushed in a westerly direction. The location today is identical to as when this scene was filmed there.

How to get there: The most direct route to this location is via train from London St Pancras Station (Lower Level) aboard a Thameslink service to Elstree and Borehamwood Station. Exit Elstree and Borehamwood Station and from Stop B board the No. 107 bus (to Edgware) and disembark at the undesignated stop (Deacon Hill Road). Turn left on Allum Lane and walk 35 metres. Turn right onto Deacons Hill Road and walk 850 metres until reaching the junction with Barnet Lane. To your left is the stretch of road with the incline and curve in the road where the motorbike and sidecar is filmed being pushed uphill.

Then

Now

The broken down motorbike is pushed up this inclining road.

Location 171: Holiday Village Road Sign

Film: *Holiday on the Buses*

St Asaph Road, Rhuddlan, Denbighshire, LL18 5UG.

On their way to the holiday camp, the family on the motorbike and sidecar speed past a sign by the side of a dual carriageway claiming it to be two miles to the Holiday Village (14 minutes 56 seconds into the film). A slip road can be seen to the left with telegraph poles by the roadside, whilst to the right is a grassy verge as the dual carriageway turns sharply right. This scene was filmed on St Asaph Road (also known as the A525) heading southwards just south of the town of Rhuddlan. Directly adjacent to where the motorbike passes the sign now is a lay-by and small hut-like structure to the left and to the right side of the road is the entrance to Blairmore House. The location today is much the same aside from a turning point in the central reservation seen in the film, which has now been replaced by a continuous grass-covered central reservation.

How to get there: The most direct route to this location from Prestatyn Station is to exit the station via the High Street exit on the right of the station. Walk 75 metres along High Street and turn right onto Bridge Road and after 45 metres turn left onto Fford Pendyffryn and cross here. From Bay 3 board the No. 13 Arriva Buses Wales service (to Llandudno Palladium). Disembark at the undesignated stop (Pengwern Meadow Brook Farm), turn left and walk 25 metres along Bodelwyddan Road. Turn right into St Asaph Road (also known as the A525) and walk 1200 metres until reaching the entrance to Blairmore House on your right. Cross onto the other side of the road onto the traffic island covered in grass with a lay-by directly alongside it for the location seen in the filming looking southwards.

Then

Now

The motorbike and sidecar passing the holiday camp sign.

Location 172: On the Approach to the Bridge

Film: *Holiday on the Buses*

High Street, Rhuddlan, Denbighshire, LL18 2UD.

From a distance, Arthur and the family aboard the motorbike and sidecar are seen being caught by Stan's bus (exactly 15 minutes into the film). The road through a small town is on a decline passing a row of stone cottages on the left and the camera filming the scene perched on a bridge further down the road. The motorbike and sidecar and bus are filmed here travelling down High Street in the small town of Rhuddlan with the bus passing No. 2 High Street on the right (out of shot) as we look at it. Today, this location has changed very little with trees and bushes being a little more prominent and the bridge on which this scene was filmed is now only accessible by traffic.

How to get there: The most direct route to this location from Prestatyn Station is to exit the station via the High Street exit on the right of the station. Walk 75 metres along High Street and turn right onto Bridge Road and after 45 metres turn left onto Fford Pendyffryn. Cross here and from Bay 3 board the No. 13 Arriva Buses Wales service (to Llandudno Palladium). Disembark at the undesignated stop (Rhuddlan Parliament House), turn right and walk 180 metres onto Station Road until halfway across the bridge marked by a protruding platform which the camera would have been perched on to film this scene.

Then

Now

Stan's bus moves to overtake the motorbike and sidecar before crossing the bridge.

Location 173: Lost Luggage

Film: *Holiday on the Buses*

The Rhuddlan Bridge, Station Road, Rhuddlan, Denbighshire, LL18 5UA.

As the motorbike and sidecar crosses a bridge, Stan's bus has to swerve to avoid colliding with a car and the motorbike is forced into the side of the bridge and the family's suitcases are ejected from the sidecar and down into the river below (15 minutes 15 seconds into the film). This scene was filmed on the Rhuddlan Bridge in Rhuddlan and the bridge today has remained much the same aside from the road over the bridge having crash barriers fitted along the westerly half of the bridge. This scene would have been filmed by the riverside looking up at the bridge and the bridge features again at the end of the film as the family head home again on the opposite side of the road and suffer an identical mishap.

How to get there: The most direct route to this location from Prestatyn Station is to exit the station via the High Street exit on the right of the station. Walk 75 metres along High Street and turn right onto Bridge Road and after 45 metres turn left onto Fford Pendyffryn. Cross here and from Bay 3 board the No. 13 Arriva Buses Wales service (to Llandudno Palladium). Disembark at the undesignated stop (Rhuddlan Parliament House), turn right and walk 190 metres until across the bridge – to your left is a grassy area by the riverbank where this scene would have been filmed.

Then

Now

The suitcases are ejected from the bridge into the river below.

Location 174: Retrieving the Cases

Film: *Holiday on the Buses*

River Clwyd, Rhuddlan Bridge, Station Road, Denbighshire, LLU 5UA.

Arthur and Olive dash down to the riverside over a rocky and muddy surface as they prepare to retrieve their luggage (15 minutes 46 seconds into the episode). On the other side of the river a grassy bank surrounding an ancient castle can be seen as Arthur and Olive stand at the foot of Rhuddlan Bridge. The river seen here is the River Clwyd as it runs below Rhuddlan Bridge and the castle seen in the background is Rhuddlan Castle. The only real difference to this scene is that the riverbank's rock and mud-strewn terrain seen in the film is now covered chiefly in grass. This scene would have been filmed further along the riverbank. Today it is impossible to recreate the view through to Rhuddlan Castle as seen in the film from the riverbank so I am presuming this scene was filmed from either a temporary jetty or the film crew in a moored boat at river level.

How to get there: The most direct route to this location from Prestatyn Station is to exit the station via the High Street exit on the right of the station. Walk 75 metres along High Street and turn right onto Bridge Road and after 45 metres turn left onto Fford Pendyffryn. Cross here and from Bay 3 board the No. 13 Arriva Buses Wales service (to Llandudno Palladium). Disembark at the undesignated stop (Rhuddlan Parliament House), turn right and walk 190 metres until across the bridge. Cross Station Road, turn right and walk ten metres to a gate on the right. Open and walk 15 metres to the riverbank and to your right at the foot of Rhuddlan Bridge is where Arthur and Olive enter the River Clwyd.

Then

Now

Arthur and Olive bid to retrieve their cases.

Location 175: The Family Arrive

Film: *Holiday on the Buses*

Barkby Avenue, Prestatyn, Denbighshire, LL19 7LA.

After a series of mishaps, Arthur, Olive, Mum and little Arthur aboard the motorbike and sidecar finally arrive at the holiday camp (16 minutes 47 seconds into the film). The vehicle turns a corner and starts on a declining road to the holiday camp gates with secure fencing lining the road on either side. This scene was filmed on Barkby Avenue and this stretch of the road is now no longer lined by secure fencing, with hedges and a smaller wooden fence now in its place.

How to get there: The most direct route to this location from Prestatyn Station is to exit the station at the Sandy Lane exit via the staircase. Walk 10 metres. turn right onto Station Road and walk for 150 metres before turning right onto Marine Road. After 500 metres cross the road and turn onto Marine Road East before turning sharply left onto Barkby Avenue. After 200 metres turn left and walk 70 metres to the gates to the holiday camp and turn around to face the direction you have travelled for the view seen in this scene.

Then

Now

The family arrive aboard the motorbike and sidecar.

Location 176: The Butler Chalet

Film: *Holiday on the Buses*

Barkby Avenue, Prestatyn, Denbighshire, LL19 7LA.

Stan leads the family, in a dishevelled state, to their chalet (17 minutes 46 seconds into the film) as they are watched by their neighbours Wally and Lily Briggs who describe them as being 'bleedin' common'. The family walk down a path along the front of a chalet block and this block remains today. The chalet is numbered 407 with the Briggs chalet now numbered 409. The window configurations and other surrounding features seen later in the film helped pinpoint this location which had been thought to have been demolished, as many blocks have been since 1973.

How to get there: The most direct route to this location from Prestatyn Station is to exit the station at the Sandy Lane exit via the staircase. Walk 10 metres, turn right onto Station Road and walk for 150 metres before turning right onto Marine Road. After 500 metres cross the road and turn onto Marine Road East before turning sharply left onto Barkby Avenue. After 200 metres turn left and walk 70 metres to the gates to the holiday camp where, to gain access to the camp, an entrance fee will apply. After a further 160 metres walk, turn right and walk for 275 metres, following this road to the right, then turn left and 20 metres to the south-west stands chalet number 407.

Then

Now

The Butler chalet today and the grass outside where Wally and Lily sit on deckchairs.

Location 177: The Bar Area

Film: *Holiday on the Buses*

Barkby Avenue, Prestatyn, Denbighshire, LL19 7LA.

The camera pans across a large bar area at the holiday camp with holidaymakers taking advantage of the entertainment (19 minutes 31 seconds into the film). The bar itself extends along the length of a wall and around a corner, with an area for seated accommodation and a dance floor also available. This scene was filmed in the main building at Pontins Prestatyn Sands holiday camp and this bar area remains to the present day, but the dance floor is now covered with more seating and tables whilst the bar itself has reduced very slightly in length. This location is seen again later in the film with Arthur flirting with another woman as he dances and as Bert plies Mum with drink.

How to get there: The most direct route to this location from Prestatyn Station is to exit the station at the Sandy Lane exit via the staircase. Walk 10 metres, turn right onto Station Road and walk for 150 metres before turning right onto Marine Road. After 500 metres cross the road and turn onto Marine Road East before turning sharply left onto Barkby Avenue. After 200 metres turn left and walk 70 metres to the gates to the holiday camp where, to gain access to the camp, an entrance fee will apply. On entering the camp, walk 180 metres to the main building's entrance and turn right into the reception area. Turn left and walk down the corridor for 10 metres, passing the Nisa store on your left and public toilets. Turn left and after five metres turn right and on your left-hand side is the bar area seen in the film.

Then

Now

The bar area as it looked in 2015.

Location 178: The Swimming Pool

Film: *Holiday on the Buses*

Barkby Avenue, Prestatyn, Denbighshire, LL19 7LA.

Stan and Jack have been designated other duties as lifeguards and are first seen being spoken to by an amazed Inspector Blake as they walk alongside an indoor swimming pool packed with holidaymakers. Olive is shortly seen walking by the poolside (21 minutes 56 seconds into the film). The swimming pool had many large glass window panes allowing in a lot of natural light and had diving boards at ground level at the top of the pool and a seated viewing area is seen in the background. Today the pool is much the same with the same tiling around the pool but the seated viewing area has been removed and replaced by benches to be used by swimmers to rest on.

How to get there: The most direct route to this location from Prestatyn Station is to exit the station at the Sandy Lane exit via the staircase. Walk 10 metres, turn right onto Station Road and walk for 150 metres before turning right onto Marine Road. After 500 metres cross the road and turn onto Marine Road East before turning sharply left onto Barkby Avenue. After 200 metres turn left and walk 70 metres to the gates to the holiday camp where, to gain access to the camp, an entrance fee will apply. On entering the camp, walk 160 metres and on your right is the swimming pool complex but access will be denied in this day and age and photography forbidden unless the pool is out of use and permission is gained from the camp manager to enter to photograph.

Then

Now

Olive is seen walking to the left of the new temporary slides in place and walks up to the steps, lined by two potted plants today, which Arthur comes up from later in the scene to confront her.

Location 179: The Mystery Tour Begins

Film: *Holiday on the Buses*

High Street, Rhyl, Denbighshire, LL18 1ET.

The holiday camp's bus is seen heading down a main street as part of a mystery tour (24 minutes 20 seconds into the film). On either side of the road are a mix of shops, cafés and banks as part of three-storey buildings in what is evidently a town centre with narrow streets. This scene was filmed on the High Street in the Welsh seaside resort of Rhyl and the bus is seen passing a Barclays Bank on the right-hand side as the bus heads northwards to the seafront. Today the Barclays Bank has relocated but the distinctive building remains on High Street on the corner of Sussex Street. The High Street section that featured in the film is now closed to traffic with market stalls now prevalent.

How to get there: The most direct route to this location from Rhyl Station is to exit the station at the Elwy Street exit. Turn right, walk 50 metres along Elwy Street and turn right onto Kinmel Street. Walk 75 metres before turning left onto High Street and walk 100 metres. On your left is the former Barclay's Bank building on the corner of Sussex Street seen as the bus passes it in the film.

Then

Now

The now pedestrianised High Street in Rhyl.

Location 180: Along the Seafront

Film: *Holiday on the Buses*

West Parade, Rhyl, Denbighshire, LL18 1HG.

With the mystery tour well underway, the holiday camp bus heads along a seafront passing a bingo hall on its right (24 minutes 29 seconds into the film). To the left of the bus, the old Rhyl Pavilion building can be seen as well as an open-air swimming pool, whilst in the foreground to the right of the bus there appears to be a hotel. This was filmed with the bus just passing the entrance to Abbey Street and today the bingo hall is now the Palace Fun Fair with the building having seen renovations, adding two protruding structures to its front. The side of this building is identifiable by the blocked up window seen on the second floor in the film and still present today, but the old Pavilion building was demolished just weeks after the film was shot here whilst the building the bus passes which was a hotel has undergone renovations and is now residential properties. Also, the zebra crossing has been replaced by a level crossing.

How to get there: The most direct route to this location from Rhyl Station is to exit the station at the Elwy Street exit. Turn left, walk 425 metres along Elwy Street and turn left into Fford Wellington. Walk 50 metres before crossing here to turn right onto Vaughan Street and walk 85 metres crossing onto Abbey Street. Walk for 230 metres and turn left into West Parade. Walk 5 metres and turn right to cross at the level crossing, turn left and walk ten metres before turning to face the direction you have come for the location shot.

Then

Now

The bus headed towards the camera amidst the mystery tour.

Location 181: Crossing a Bridge

Film: Holiday on the Buses

Rhyl Fford Harbour Bridge, Wellington Road, Rhyl, Denbighshire, LL18 5BQ.

As the mystery tour continues, the bus crosses a distinctive looking grey-painted bridge (24 minutes 39 seconds into the film). The bridge seen in the film crosses a river with boats moored to the right and a distinctive three-storey house directly at the end of the bridge with a town in the background behind it. This scene was filmed on the Fford Harbour Bridge in Rhyl, with the bus heading eastwards towards Rhyl's town centre. Today the bridge remains unchanged though is now painted bright blue and boats are still moored below in what is Rhyl Harbour. The town seen in the background is that of Kinmel Bay. The distinctive three-storey building remains and is The Harbour public house.

How to get there: The most direct route to this location from Rhyl Station is to exit the station at the Elwy Street exit. Turn right and walk 10 metres to Rhyl Bus Station and from Bay 1 board the No. 12 Arriva Buses Wales service (to Denbigh). Disembark at the undesignated stop (Marine Lake), turn right and walk 250 metres and directly ahead is the Rhyl Fford Harbour Bridge that the bus is seen crossing heading eastwards.

Then

Now

The bridge crossed during the mystery tour.

Location 182: The Waterfall Stop

Film: *Holiday on the Buses*

Dyserth Falls, Waterfall Road, Dyserth, Denbighshire, LL18 6ET.

Stan and Jack walk across a grassy area in conversation and are keen to urge their passengers to board the bus as Stan frets about missing a date with a holidaymaker (24 minutes 44 seconds into the film). A waterfall can be seen in the background with a grassy area with round tables with parasols scattered around, with passengers from the mystery tour sitting around them. This scene was filmed at the local beauty spot of Dyserth Falls in the small town of Dyserth, a few miles to the south-west of Prestatyn. The popular visitors' attraction remains much unchanged to the present day, with the waterfall still present of course as is the vast grassy area, but the round tables and chairs have been replaced by wooden benches attached to wooden tables for seating.

How to get there: The most direct route to this location from Prestatyn Station is to exit the station via the High Street exit on the right of the station. Walk 75 metres along High Street and turn right onto Bridge Road and after 45 metres turn left onto Fford Pendyffryn. Cross here and from Bay 2 board the No. 35 Arriva Buses Wales service (to Rhyl Bus Station). Disembark at the undesignated stop (Dyserth Carreg Heilin), turn right and walk 175 metres along Waterfall Road (also known as the B5119) and on your left is Dyserth Falls. Turn left, walk 50 metres and cross the bridge, turn left and walk 10 metres to the south-west for roughly the place where this scene was filmed.

Then

Now

The Dyserth Waterfall visited in *Holiday on the Buses*.

Location 183: Blakey Buys Joan an Ice Cream

Film: *Holiday on the Buses*

Dyserth Falls, Waterfall Road, Dyserth, Denbighshire, LL18 6ET.

During the stop on the mystery tour, Blakey is seen exiting a shop with two ice creams, one of which he hands to Joan (25 minutes 39 seconds into the film). The shop with a black wooden door had a green metal fence adjacent, which was ajar, with a path in the background lined by a hedge. This was filmed at the side entrance into a shop at Dyserth Falls and the shop remains to this day virtually unchanged. The wooden black door is still present but the gate, although identical in design, is now painted black and the path and hedge in the background can still be seen today.

How to get there: The most direct route to this location from Prestatyn Station is to exit the station via the High Street exit on the right of the station. Walk 75 metres along High Street and turn right onto Bridge Road and after 45 metres turn left onto Fford Pendyffryn. Cross here and from Bay 2 board the No. 35 Arriva Buses Wales service (to Rhyl Bus Station). Disembark at the undesignated stop (Dyserth Carreg Heilin), turn right and walk 175 metres along Waterfall Road (also known as the B5119) and on your left is Dyserth Falls. Turn left and walk 5 metres until almost adjacent with the side door to the shop where Blakey is seen exiting in this scene.

Then

Now

Blakey exited this door to hand Joan her ice cream.

Location 184: Olive Exits a Shop in a Rush

Film: *Holiday on the Buses*

The Waterfall Shop, Waterfall Road, Dyserth, Denbighshire, LL18 6ET.

Stan calls for Olive to hurry up as he grows impatient to resume the mystery tour and she rushes out of a shop carrying candy floss (26 minutes 39 seconds into the film). The shop is made of stone which is painted white with black cornering, with boxes of chocolates, jars of sweets and bottles of juice visible in the shop window and a bubble gum machine outside. This was filmed at the shop located at Dyserth Falls at the entrance into the tourist attraction. The location today remains unchanged although the bubble gum machine is no longer present, with a small post box now to the far left of the shop front, whilst the shop window has an array of ornaments and cuddly toys on display and a neon sign sits centrally in the window.

How to get there: The most direct route to this location from Prestatyn Station is to exit the station via the High Street exit on the right of the station. Walk 75 metres along High Street and turn right onto Bridge Road and after 45 metres turn left onto Fford Pendyffryn. Cross here and from Bay 2 board the No. 35 Arriva Buses Wales service (to Rhyl Bus Station). Disembark at the undesignated stop (Dyserth Carreg Heilin), turn right and walk 175 metres along Waterfall Road (also known as the B5119) and on your left is Dyserth Falls. Walk 5 metres until just left of the shop with the correct angle for when Olive rushes from the shop in the film.

Then

Now

The shop that Olive exits in a hurry with her candy floss.

Location 185: Taking a U-turn on the Motorway

Film: *Holiday on the Buses*

St Asaph Road, Rhuddlan, Denbighshire, LL18 5UG.

The mystery tour bus speeds along a motorway before taking a U-turn, passing through a gap in the grass-covered central reservation (27 minutes 5 seconds into the film). The bus turns on a slight bend in the motorway with fields on both side of the road with a telegraph pole at the roadside where the bus turns. This location was filmed on St Asaph Road and today the bus would have been unable to do this manoeuvre as the central reservation (still grass covered) is now continuous with no break in it. The bus had just passed what is now Blairmore House, heading north towards Rhuddlan and turned at the second telegraph pole past Blairmore House. The telegraph poles are still in place at this location and this scene would have been filmed from the opposite side of the road, almost opposite Blairmore House.

How to get there: The most direct route to this location from Prestatyn Station is to exit the station via the High Street exit on the right of the station. Walk 75 metres along High Street and turn right onto Bridge Road and after 45 metres turn left onto Fford Pendyffryn. Cross here and from Bay 3 board the No. 13 Arriva Buses Wales service (to Llandudno Palladium). Disembark at the undesignated stop (Pengwern Meadow Brook Farm), turn left and walk 25 metres along Bodelwyddan Road. Turn right into St Asaph Road (also known as the A525) and walk 1150 metres until reaching a gate on your right. Cross onto the other side of the road onto the traffic island covered in grass with a lay-by directly alongside and turn to look north. The second telegraph pole along the roadside is where the bus does its U-turn.

Then

Now

The U-turn would not be possible today due to a central reservation in place.

On The Buses: The Filming Locations

Location 186: Heading down a Country Lane

Film: *Holiday on the Buses*

Unnamed Lane off St Asaph Road, Rhuddlan, Denbighshire, LL18 5UG.

Moments after its U-turn on the motorway the bus turns sharply left down a tree-lined country lane (27 minutes 20 seconds into the film). The lane curves off to the left and the entrance to the lane has a brick wall on the left and hedge on the right with grass- and dirt-covered verges by the roadside. This scene was filmed on St Asaph Road with the bus turning off the road directly across the dual carriageway from Blairmore House. Today, hedges can be seen on both sides of the lane and the grass and dirt verges on the edge of the lane's entrance have been replaced by a cycle path. Trees and hedges still line the unnamed lane with road signs now on both sides of the road as you enter the lane.

How to get there: The most direct route to this location from Prestatyn Station is to exit the station via the High Street exit on the right of the station. Walk 75 metres along High Street and turn right onto Bridge Road and after 45 metres turn left onto Fford Pendyffryn. Cross here and from Bay 3 board the No. 13 Arriva Buses Wales service (to Llandudno Palladium). Disembark at the undesignated stop (Pengwern Meadow Brook Farm), turn left and walk 25 metres along Bodelwyddan Road. Turn right into St Asaph Road (also known as the A525) and walk 1150 metres until reaching a gate on your right. Cross onto the other side of the road onto the traffic island covered in grass with a lay-by directly alongside and straight ahead is the country lane the bus travels down.

Then

Now

The country lane which was part of the mystery tour.

Location 187: Low-Level Bridge

Film: *Holiday on the Buses*

Allt Y Graig, Dyserth, Denbighshire, LL18 6DE.

The bus turns into a narrow country lane lined by steep banks and trees with a low-level railway bridge ahead (27 minutes 36 seconds into the film). The bridge straddles the road below as it turns sharply left, with trees, bushes and hedges on steep banks along the roadside. This scene was filmed on the rural Allt Y Graig in the hills above the town of Dyserth. This filming location has hardly changed at all, with the surrounding landscape identical, with the only discernible difference being the fence that runs along the top of the bridge. The white fencing has been replaced by a wooden fence more akin to those seen in gardens. Also, white lines have now been painted around the outside edges of the narrow road since this scene was filmed here.

How to get there: The most direct route to this location from Prestatyn Station is to exit the station via the High Street exit on the right of the station. Walk 75 metres along High Street and turn right onto Bridge Road and after 45 metres turn left onto Fford Pendyffryn. Cross here and from Bay 2 board the No. 35 Arriva Buses Wales service (to Rhyl Bus Station). Disembark at the undesignated stop (Meliden Fford Ty Newydd), turn right and walk 180 metres along Fford Talargoch. Turn left onto Allt Y Graig to walk 200 metres up a steeply inclining road until reaching the other side of the railway bridge and at the bend on the road is where this scene was filmed. Beware though as this location has no pavements as such so please mind the traffic.

Then

Now

The low-level bridge that causes chaos on the upper deck.

Location 188: Overhanging Trees Play Havoc

Film: *Holiday on the Buses*

Allt Y Graig, Dyserth, Denbighshire, LL18 6DE.

Turning sharply left along a country lane lined with trees with overhanging branches the passengers on the open upper deck of the bus duck for cover (28 minutes 7 seconds into the film). The overhanging trees causing the havoc were on the left-hand side of the road, whilst trees are in evidence on the right-hand side of the road and up ahead an old stone wall around ten-foot high to the right curves around the bend in the road with a telegraph pole visible. This scene was filmed on Allt Y Graig around 175 metres to the south of the railway bridge seen seconds earlier, with the bus heading in the opposite direction now. Today this location is much the same with the stone wall still present as is the telegraph pole and overhanging trees to the left. This location is a few metres south of Craig Y Castell Lodge on Allt Y Graig.

How to get there: The most direct route to this location from Prestatyn Station is to exit the station via the High Street exit on the right of the station. Walk 75 metres along High Street and turn right onto Bridge Road and after 45 metres turn left onto Fford Pendyffryn. Cross here and from Bay 2 board the No. 35 Arriva Buses Wales service (to Rhyl Bus Station). Disembark at the undesignated stop (Meliden Fford Ty Newydd), turn right and walk 180 metres along Fford Talargoch. Turn left onto Allt Y Graig to walk 350 metres up a steeply inclining and winding road until reaching a left bend in the road with the stone wall banking the road on the right just ahead. Beware though as this location has no pavements as such so please mind the traffic.

Then

Now

The overhanging trees are still evident today.

Location 189: Removing the Branches

Film: *Holiday on the Buses*

Allt Y Graig, Dyserth, Denbighshire, LL18 6DE.

Jack moves along the top deck of the bus removing branches as it moves along a country lane (28 minutes 22 seconds into the film). In the background, a large distinctively-shaped house painted white can be seen to the left of a cluster of tall trees and the narrow lane the bus passes along is lined by hedges. This scene filmed the bus travelling westwards along Allt Y Graig with the house in the background standing at the junction of Allt Y Graig and Pandy Lane. The location today is much the same with the house in the background largely unchanged and the trees still present, although the hedges that run alongside the lane have grown somewhat.

How to get there: The most direct route to this location from Prestatyn Station is to exit the station via the High Street exit on the right of the station. Walk 75 metres along High Street and turn right onto Bridge Road and after 45 metres turn left onto Fford Pendyffryn. Cross here and from Bay 2 board the No. 35 Arriva Buses Wales service (to Rhyl Bus Station). Disembark at the undesignated stop (Meliden Fford Ty Newydd), turn right and walk 180 metres along Fford Talargoch. Turn left onto Allt Y Graig to walk 530 metres up a steeply inclining and winding road until just after passing a house on your right with a telegraph pole adjacent on your right, where this scene would have been shot with the house seen in the background in the distance.

Then

Now

The house in the distance is today masked by trees and bushes somewhat.

Location 190: Stan Visits Mavis in her Chalet

Film: *Holiday on the Buses*

Barkby Avenue, Prestatyn, Denbighshire, LL19 7LA.

After racing to complete the mystery tour, Stan rushes up a flight of stairs and knocks on the chalet door belonging to Mavis (28 minutes 32 seconds into the film). The chalet, located on an upper floor has an adjacent chalet block in the background and to the rear of that the rear of another chalet block can be seen. Today this chalet is numbered 390, but the surrounding chalet blocks seen in the film have long since been demolished. However, it can be identified by the side-on chalet block also seen in the film which remains to this day. The chalet block used here was directly opposite that used for the Butler and Briggs chalets and the exploding drains scene so it is safe to presume that this section of the camp was used for filming extensively.

How to get there: The most direct route to this location from Prestatyn Station is to exit the station at the Sandy Lane exit via the staircase. Walk 10 metres, turn right onto Station Road and walk for 150 metres before turning right onto Marine Road. After 500 metres cross the road and turn onto Marine Road East before turning sharply left onto Barkby Avenue. After 200 metres turn left and walk 70 metres to the gates to the holiday camp where, to gain access to the camp, an entrance fee will apply. After a further 180-metre walk, turn right after passing the swimming pool. Walk for 250 metres following this road to the right, turn left and walk 5 metres to stairs that lead up to the chalet numbered 390.

Then

Now

Stan knocks on this chalet door on his visit to Mavis only to be foiled yet again.

Location 191: Dance Rehearsals

Film: *Holiday on the Buses*

Barkby Avenue, Prestatyn, Denbighshire, LL19 7LA.

Inspector Blake is seen calling everyone to gather around in a vast dance hall with people seated and others standing around (29 minutes 19 seconds into the film). The dance hall has a stage in the background with a piano positioned in the centre of the floor, especially for this scene with wooden flooring. A seated area can be seen to the far right. This scene was filmed in the ballroom at the holiday camp and this facility remains on site to this day. The only changes to this area are that a wall and windows separate the cafeteria area from the ballroom. The décor today has changed from the orange seen in the film to darker colours today. This location features later in the film when the exhibition of old time dancing and The Farewell Ball is held here.

How to get there: The most direct route to this location from Prestatyn Station is to exit the station at the Sandy Lane exit via the staircase. Walk 10 metres, turn right onto Station Road and walk for 150 metres before turning right onto Marine Road. After 500 metres cross the road and turn onto Marine Road East before turning sharply left onto Barkby Avenue. After 200 metres turn left and walk 70 metres to the gates to the holiday camp where, to gain access to the camp, an entrance fee will apply. On entering the camp, walk 180 metres to the main building's entrance and turn right into the reception area. Turn left and walk down the corridor for 10 metres passing the Nisa store on your left and public toilets. Turn left and after five metres turn right and twenty metres to your right is the ballroom seen in the film.

Then

Now

The ballroom with the same globular lamps seen in the film hanging from the ceiling.

Location 192: Exiting the Amusement Arcade

Film: *Holiday on the Buses*

Barkby Avenue, Prestatyn, Denbighshire, LL19 7LA.

Mum and Bert are seen at a shooting gallery in an amusement arcade before they exit and walk out into the reception area watched by Stan and Jack (39 minutes 4 seconds into the film). This amusement arcade was located where, today, a small coffee shop equipped with video games called the Java Lounge now stands with a door leading into the reception area today, which has been greatly redeveloped since 1973 when the film was shot here. One clue remains in that Mum and Bert walk past a pillar which still stands in the reception area today.

How to get there: The most direct route to this location from Prestatyn Station is to exit the station at the Sandy Lane exit via the staircase. Walk 10 metres, turn right onto Station Road and walk for 150 metres before turning right onto Marine Road. After 500 metres cross the road and turn onto Marine Road East before turning sharply left onto Barkby Avenue. After 200 metres turn left and walk 70 metres to the gates to the holiday camp where, to gain access to the camp, an entrance fee will apply. On entering the camp, walk 180 metres to the main building's entrance on your right and enter the reception area and the Java Lounge is on your right.

Then

Now

The pillar which Mum and Bert are seen passing and the door to the right is seen in the film on the other side of the reception desk when it was positioned there in 1973.

Location 193: The Waiting Room

Film: *Holiday on the Buses*

Barkby Avenue, Prestatyn, Denbighshire, LL19 7LA.

Jack, faking a limp, enters the first aid room and takes a seat in the waiting room (48 minutes 16 seconds into the film). The waiting room is a small area with a handful of seats dotted around and a corridor to the right which has treatment rooms leading off of it. This was the camp's first aid facility when *Holiday on the Buses* was filmed here but today this area is now put to a different use, with the dividing walls knocked down. The last time I was able to gain access to it in 2015 it was used to store the camp tricycles, some of which were in need of repair. This location features again later in the film. If you do intend on visiting it is worth knowing that you may not gain access to this area of the camp.

How to get there: The most direct route to this location from Prestatyn Station is to exit the station at the Sandy Lane exit via the staircase. Walk 10 metres, turn right onto Station Road and walk for 150 metres before turning right onto Marine Road. After 500 metres cross the road and turn onto Marine Road East before turning sharply left onto Barkby Avenue. After 200 metres turn left and walk 70 metres to the gates to the holiday camp where, to gain access to the camp, an entrance fee will apply. On entering the camp, walk 100 metres and to your right is the single-storey block where the door to the far left was the entrance to the first aid room. What was the waiting room is on the other side of this door but is now locked and permission has to be attained to gain access to this area.

Then

Now

The seated waiting area was once situated here – note the unchanged windows to the left.

Location 194: The Treatment Room

Film: *Holiday on the Buses*

Barkby Avenue, Prestatyn, Denbighshire, LL19 7LA.

Jack first enters the nurse's treatment room for a moment of passion (48 minutes 36 seconds into the film). The walls are painted a pale yellow with a set of narrow windows set high up the wall with medical equipment scattered around. This location is seen again later in the film when Stan receives treatment and later when Jack exits the room in a hurry via one of the rear windows. Today this room has had its dividing walls knocked down and is now one large storage space that includes the former waiting room and corridor. It is now used to store tricycles and bicycles. If you visit you will need permission to gain access to this building.

How to get there: The most direct route to this location from Prestatyn Station is to exit the station at the Sandy Lane exit via the staircase. Walk 10 metres, turn right onto Station Road and walk for 150 metres before turning right onto Marine Road. After 500 metres cross the road and turn onto Marine Road East before turning sharply left onto Barkby Avenue. After 200 metres turn left and walk 70 metres to the gates to the holiday camp where, to gain access to the camp, an entrance fee will apply. On entering the camp, walk 100 metres and to your right is the single-storey block where the door to the far left was the entrance to the first aid room. On the other side of this door, which is now permanently locked, is the waiting room, corridor and treatment rooms but all walls have been knocked down to create one large storage area.

Then

Now

The treatment rooms and the window to the left of the piled up tyres is where Jack makes his hasty exit later in the film.

Location 195: The Exploding Drains

Film: *Holiday on the Buses*

Barkby Avenue, Prestatyn, Denbighshire, LL19 7LA.

As Blakey makes his way through the holiday camp, with a chalet block in the background and a view through to the rear of the main building (50 minutes 31 seconds into the film), the drains blow up, knocking the inspector off his feet. This scene was filmed with the block containing the Butler and Briggs chalets to Blakey's left as we look at it. Many of the external camp shots were filmed in this block and it can be presumed that this area of the camp was hired for filming.

How to get there: The most direct route to this location from Prestatyn Station is to exit the station at the Sandy Lane exit via the staircase. Walk 10 metres, turn right onto Station Road and walk for 150 metres before turning right onto Marine Road. After 500 metres cross the road and turn onto Marine Road East before turning sharply left onto Barkby Avenue. After 200 metres turn left and walk 70 metres to the gates to the holiday camp where, to gain access to the camp, an entrance fee will apply. After a further 180-metre walk, turn right and walk for 275 metres following this road to the right and turn left to walk 50 metres to the south-west to where chalet blocks numbering 377 to 388 meet the south end of chalet block numbering 401 to 412. Look south-west through the gap between the chalet blocks for the angle seen in the film.

Then

Now

The drains that exploded in the film remain (just out of shot) beyond the chalet blocks in the forefront.

Location 196: Stan, Jack and a Toilet

Film: *Holiday on the Buses*

Barkby Avenue, Prestatyn, Denbighshire, LL19 7LA.

In semi-darkness, Stan and Jack carry a toilet taken from the camp stores through the holiday camp (55 minutes 52 seconds into the film). This scene was filmed in the north part of the centre circular area of the holiday camp with the camera following them as they pass a servicing block on their right, which are seen scattered throughout the camp to the present day. To Jack's left is the block today that holds chalet numbers 401 to 412 and this can be ascertained as the chalet blocks in the background all tally up perfectly with what stands there in the present day.

How to get there: The most direct route to this location from Prestatyn Station is to exit the station at the Sandy Lane exit via the staircase. Walk 10 metres, turn right onto Station Road and walk for 150 metres before turning right onto Marine Road. After 500 metres cross the road and turn onto Marine Road East before turning sharply left onto Barkby Avenue. After 200 metres turn left and walk 70 metres to the gates to the holiday camp where, to gain access to the camp, an entrance fee will apply. On entering the camp, walk 180 metres and take your first turn right along the road after passing the swimming pool. Walk 90 metres before turning right following the road around for 250 metres until reaching a service station. Turn left and walk 10 metres until at the north end of the chalet block with chalets numbered 401 to 412 for the filming location, looking westwards.

Then

Now

**Stan and Jack carry the toilet here in semi-darkness,
heading from right to left.**

Location 197: Wally Leads Lily to the Toilet in the Bushes

Film: *Holiday on the Buses*

Barkby Avenue, Prestatyn, Denbighshire, LL19 7LA.

Wally is startled when he finds a toilet in the bushes and gets Lily to have a look, leading her up a path from their chalet (56 minutes 23 seconds into the film). In the background, over the top of the adjacent chalet block which runs parallel to theirs, can be seen the top of the Clwydian range of hills that run to the south of Prestatyn. This is the only such block in the camp that affords such a view and was a big help in pinpointing the Butler and Briggs chalet block. The block today remains much the same aside from some cosmetic changes to the chalets such as new paintwork.

How to get there: The most direct route to this location from Prestatyn Station is to exit the station at the Sandy Lane exit via the staircase. Walk 10 metres, turn right onto Station Road and walk for 150 metres before turning right onto Marine Road. After 500 metres cross the road and turn onto Marine Road East before turning sharply left onto Barkby Avenue. After 200 metres turn left and walk 70 metres to the gates to the holiday camp where, to gain access to the camp, an entrance fee will apply. After a further 180-metre walk, turn right after passing the swimming pool. Walk for 275 metres following this road to the right, then turn left and 20 metres to the south-west stands the path Wally and Lily walk up outside their chalet.

Then

Now

**Wally leads Lily up the path to the far right with the
Clwydian hills visible in the distance.**

Location 198: The Manager's House

Film: *Holiday on the Buses*

Hillside, Prestatyn, Denbighshire, LL19 9PW.

As Stan attempts to escape the manager's house via a milk hatch in the back door, the pet dog tries squeezing through at the same time as Maria comes to his rescue along a path in the back garden of the house (64 minutes 11 seconds into the film) and is the only external shot we see of the house. A paved garden path that Maria walks along runs adjacent to the rear of the property and to the right is an elaborate rock garden with steps visible in the foreground. This scene was filmed at a property on Hillside in Prestatyn, which runs along the side of the Clwydian Hills that overlook the town of Prestatyn. Today the property's garden remains pretty much unchanged but the paving slabs that made up the path have been replaced by a gravel path.

How to get there: The most direct route to this location from Prestatyn Station is to exit the station via the High Street exit on the right of the station. Walk 75 metres along High Street and turn right onto Bridge Road and after 45 metres turn left onto Fford Pendyffryn. Cross here and from Bay 3 board the No. 13 Arriva Buses Wales service (Llandudno). Disembark at the undesignated stop (St Elmo's Drive – SW Bound), turn left to walk along Meliden Road for 90 metres before turning right into Bryntirion Drive. Walk 350 metres and turn left into Upper Bryntirion Drive, walking for a further 110 metres. Turn left into Stoneby Drive and walk 30 metres before turning right into Orme View Road to walk for 50 metres. Turn left into Manor Close and walk 125 metres before turning sharp right into Bishopswood Road. Walk 35 metres before turning left into Hillside and keep left to walk 110 metres up the inclining Hillside to a junction. The small drive to your right leads up to the property, which was the manager's house, after a further 40-metre walk. Bear in mind this is private property so permission must be obtained to visit and photograph this property.

Then

Now

Stan tried escaping through a milk hatch at a specially-fitted door where the current door in the foreground of shot now stands.

Location 199: Mr Coombs Berates Inspector Blake

Film: *Holiday on the Buses*

Barkby Avenue, Prestatyn, Denbighshire, LL19 7LA.

As Mr Coombs walks through the camp alongside Inspector Blake, he berates him for making unfounded allegations about staff (70 minutes 41 seconds into the film). In the background to their left is the camp's swimming pool with a small flight of steps leading up into it, whilst running alongside the front of the building was a bench and a grassy verge can be seen to their right. This scene was filmed just outside the swimming pool and today the grassy verge and path remain but the bench has been removed and replaced by a ramp allowing wheelchair access to the pool, whilst the small flight of stairs remain.

How to get there: The most direct route to this location from Prestatyn Station is to exit the station at the Sandy Lane exit via the staircase. Walk 10 metres, turn right onto Station Road and walk for 150 metres before turning right onto Marine Road. After 500 metres cross the road and turn onto Marine Road East before turning sharply left onto Barkby Avenue. After 200 metres turn left and walk 70 metres to the gates to the holiday camp where, to gain access to the camp, an entrance fee will apply. On entering the camp, walk 155 metres and on passing the former first aid room on your right, turn right and walk 10 metres and to your right is the swimming pool complex where this scene was filmed.

Then

Now

Blakey is chastised by Mr Coombs as they walk past the front of the swimming pool.

Location 200: Blakey Confronts Stan

Film: *Holiday on the Buses*

Barkby Avenue, Prestatyn, Denbighshire, LL19 7LA.

Stan adjusts his tie as he is about to be confronted by an angry Blakey in the camp, with the east side wall of the swimming pool in the background (71 minutes 57 seconds into the film). The brown-bricked wall remains unchanged and the lamp post in the background remains in the same place with, in the distance, the two houses still remaining but they have undergone redevelopment to the roofs and their chimney arrangements and are now slightly masked by a tree which has grown over the years. This scene would have been filmed at the rear of what was then the first aid rooms where a children's play area once stood.

How to get there: The most direct route to this location from Prestatyn Station is to exit the station at the Sandy Lane exit via the staircase. Walk 10 metres, turn right onto Station Road and walk for 150 metres before turning right onto Marine Road. After 500 metres cross the road and turn onto Marine Road East before turning sharply left onto Barkby Avenue. After 200 metres turn left and walk 70 metres to the gates to the holiday camp where, to gain access to the camp, an entrance fee will apply. On entering the camp, walk 155 metres and, on passing the former first aid room on your right, turn right and walk 20 metres to the rear of the former first aid rooms with the east side of the swimming pool to your left where this scene was filmed.

Then

Now

Stan was confronted by Blakey at this location.

Location 201: The Boating Lake

Film: *Holiday on the Buses*

Barkby Avenue, Prestatyn, Denbighshire, LL19 7LA.

As Stan asks what he has done as he stands at the edge of a boating lake, Blakey prods him with his walking stick (72 minutes 33 seconds into the film). The boating lake has pedal boats in evidence and to the left of shot the east side of the swimming pool can be seen and to the right a chalet block. This scene was filmed around 50 metres north of the first aid rooms and today the boating lake has been drained of water and is now used as a go-karting track with a blue three-foot high metal fence surrounding the track. Aside from the indoor skate park under the white tarpaulin which blocks out the view to the swimming pool, the surrounding buildings have remained unchanged since this scene was filmed there

How to get there: The most direct route to this location from Prestatyn Station is to exit the station at the Sandy Lane exit via the staircase. Walk 10 metres, turn right onto Station Road and walk for 150 metres before turning right onto Marine Road. After 500 metres cross the road and turn onto Marine Road East before turning sharply left onto Barkby Avenue. After 200 metres turn left and walk 70 metres to the gates to the holiday camp where, to gain access to the camp, an entrance fee will apply. On entering the camp, walk 155 metres and, on passing the former first aid room on your right, turn right and walk 20 metres to the rear of the former first aid rooms with the east side of the swimming pool to your left. Walk 50 metres to the edge of the boating lake looking west where this scene was filmed.

Then

Now

Blakey prods Stan in the chest with his walking stick.

Location 202: *Exiting the Boating Lake*

Film: Holiday on the Buses

Barkby Avenue, Prestatyn, Denbighshire, LL19 7LA.

Stan, after being chased through the boating lake, is helped out of it by a little boy (73 minutes 23 seconds into the film). A concrete path surrounds the lake with grassy verges stretching back to a chalet in the background which has a bench in front of it and a newly-planted tree. Stan exits the lake at a point where a path heads off in a north-easterly direction. The boating lake today has been drained of water and is now used as a go-karting track, whilst there is a blue three-foot high metal fence surrounding the track and the path around it. The path Stan heads off in a north-easterly direction remains as does the chalet block which has undergone renovation and the tree has now grown somewhat in size.

How to get there: The most direct route to this location from Prestatyn Station is to exit the station at the Sandy Lane exit via the staircase. Walk 10 metres, turn right onto Station Road and walk for 150 metres before turning right onto Marine Road. After 500 metres cross the road and turn onto Marine Road East before turning sharply left onto Barkby Avenue. After 200 metres turn left and walk 70 metres to the gates to the holiday camp where, to gain access to the camp, an entrance fee will apply. On entering the camp, walk 155 metres and, on passing the former first aid room on your right, turn right and walk 20 metres to the rear of the former first aid rooms with the east side of the swimming pool to your left. Walk 50 metres to the edge of the boating lake and walk to the east side of the pool. Look across to the north end of the former boating lake to where a path heads in a north-easterly direction for the point that Stan exits the lake in the film.

Then

Now

The path Stan runs up can just be seen here.

Location 203: The Chase Continues

Film: *Holiday on the Buses*

Barkby Avenue, Prestatyn, Denbighshire, LL19 7LA.

The chase continues through the camp as Stan runs past Mr Coombs with Blakey limping along behind (73 minutes 25 seconds into the film). Stan runs through an area with chalet blocks all around, having just passed a flower bed and crossing a grass-covered space between chalet blocks with a small service station to the right. Today the area has changed as the grass has been replaced by a road allowing access to chalets with holidaymakers travelling by car, but much else is as was in the film. This shot was taken with Stan having just passed a chalet block containing chalet numbers 17 to 28 on his left. This location is also where Joan rushes across, bumping into Blakey who falls on top of her, tearing her uniform as he tries to get her off him with Mr Coombs watching on.

How to get there: The most direct route to this location from Prestatyn Station is to exit the station at the Sandy Lane exit via the staircase. Walk 10 metres, turn right onto Station Road and walk for 150 metres before turning right onto Marine Road. After 500 metres cross the road and turn onto Marine Road East before turning sharply left onto Barkby Avenue. After 200 metres turn left and walk 70 metres to the gates to the holiday camp where, to gain access to the camp, an entrance fee will apply. On entering the camp, walk 155 metres and, on passing the former first aid room on your right, turn right and walk 20 metres to the rear of the former first aid rooms with the east side of the swimming pool to your left. Walk 80 metres until reaching a path heading north-east from the go-karting area. Walk along this path for 20 metres until adjacent with the east side of a chalet block and look ahead to the road behind the chalet where Stan is seen running.

Then

Now

The newly-planted plants in 1973 have grown into bushes of fair size.

Location 204: Sacked

Film: *Holiday on the Buses*

Barkby Avenue, Prestatyn, Denbighshire, LL19 7LA.

Mr Coombs pulls Blakey off of Joan and has no alternative but to sack him for his conduct (73 minutes 50 seconds into the film). In the background is the rear of a block of chalets with a staircase running up the side, leading to the upper floor chalets. A fire hydrant can be seen on the wall, whilst Blakey and Mr Coombs stand on a grass-covered area. This scene was filmed at the rear of the east end of the chalet block which today contains chalets numbered 109 to 120. Today the grass surface has been replaced by a road but the chalets remain unchanged.

How to get there: The most direct route to this location from Prestatyn Station is to exit the station at the Sandy Lane exit via the staircase. Walk 10 metres, turn right onto Station Road and walk for 150 metres before turning right onto Marine Road. After 500 metres cross the road and turn onto Marine Road East before turning sharply left onto Barkby Avenue. After 200 metres turn left and walk 70 metres to the gates to the holiday camp where, to gain access to the camp, an entrance fee will apply. On entering the camp, walk 155 metres and, on passing the former first aid room on your right, turn right and walk 20 metres to the rear of the former first aid rooms with the east side of the swimming pool to your left. Walk 80 metres until reaching a path heading north-east from the go-karting area. Walk along this path for 20 metres until adjacent with the east side of a chalet block (containing chalets 109 to 120) and continue to walk five metres until you are at a roadside. Directly ahead on your left is the rear of the chalet block where Blakey is sacked.

Then

Now

The location where the unfortunate Blakey is sacked.

Location 205: The Beached Bus

Film: *Holiday on the Buses*

Barkby Beach, Prestatyn, Denbighshire, LL19 7LB.

After taking the bus on a moonlight mystery tour especially for two holidaymakers, Stan and Jack push their luck too far when the bus gets beached in wet sand and they cannot move it even when pushed by Jack and their dates (80 minutes and 40 seconds into the film). On the hills in the background there is a lone white house, whilst look closely and a television transmitter can be seen and each are still present today at this location. This scene was filmed on Barkby Beach less than half a mile from the Pontins holiday camp and access onto the beach was available via a ramp still present to this day in front of the Prestatyn Sailing Club. Coastal defences in the form of boulders have since been added to the location, slightly altering its appearance, but the rolling hills and white house in the background remain.

How to get there: The most direct route to this location from Prestatyn Station is to exit the station at the Sandy Lane exit via the staircase. Walk 10 metres, turn right onto Station Road and walk for 150 metres before turning right onto Marine Road. After 500 metres cross the road and turn onto Marine Road East before turning sharply left onto Barkby Avenue. After 510 metres turn right and walk 30 metres to the gates to the Prestatyn Sailing Club building on Barkby Beach. Continue to walk east for 50 metres along the coastline and turn left to walk down the ramp used by the bus onto the beach. Walk straight ahead for 100 metres (only if the tide is out of course) and turn to face the coastline for the location of the beached bus.

Then

Now

The marking in the sand denotes where the bus would have been parked.

Location 206: Checking on the Beached Bus

Film: *Holiday on the Buses*

Barkby Beach, Prestatyn, Denbighshire, LL19 7LB.

Stan and Jack clamber up a steep bank to check on their bus which had earlier become beached in wet sand (80 minutes 53 seconds into the film). In the background to the right in the distance the east side of the Pontins Prestatyn Sands holiday camp can be seen, whilst directly behind them is a golf course with the hills overlooking Prestatyn behind that. From these clues it can be deduced that this scene was filmed to the east of the holiday camp and the golf course behind them is the Prestatyn Golf Club course. This scene was filmed roughly 400 metres east of the Prestatyn Sailing Club located on Barkby Beach and the reinforcement of the coastline has seen the sand dunes replaced by a grassy bank.

How to get there: The most direct route to this location from Prestatyn Station is to exit the station at the Sandy Lane exit via the staircase. Walk 10 metres, turn right onto Station Road and walk for 150 metres before turning right onto Marine Road. After 500 metres cross the road and turn onto Marine Road East before turning sharply left onto Barkby Avenue. After 510 metres turn right and walk 30 metres to the gates to the Prestatyn Sailing Club building on Barkby Beach. Continue to walk east for 400 metres along the coastline with the beach on your left and a steep bank to your right. This point is where we see Stan and Jack clambering up the bank to check on the beached bus in the film.

Then

Now

Stan and Jack climbed this bank and to the far right the holiday camp can be seen.

Chapter Four – The Ones That Got Away

It was inevitable that some filming locations were to prove impossible to locate. The reasons for this vary, as some simply do not offer up enough clues, whilst others may be in areas that have been totally redeveloped. Also, rural locations proved very difficult to pinpoint as trees and country lanes everywhere do tend to look very similar, which leaves you with the problem of where do you start looking for such a location? Also, some locations that are known but never made the book were omitted as certain areas have changed beyond recognition and photographing them would not give you that connection with the location. In this chapter I will briefly go over those locations that have managed to frustratingly avoid detection or evaded inclusion in the book.

In the fourth episode in Series One, *Bus Driver's Stomach*, Stan gets out of his cab to blow up his rubber ring at what looks like a street lined by shops. We get the glimpse of a shop selling children's prams in the background but no view of the window configuration above the shop to help. I believe this location may be in the Wembley area.

The fifth episode in Series One, *The New Inspector*, sees Stan getting splashed by a bus as it passes him by at a bus stop. We see what looks like an office or factory type building in the background and I'd say this location was in Wood Green.

Finally, in Series One, in the episode, *The Canteen*, Stan and Jack drink from a stream at the bottom of a steep embankment by the side of a country road. Although this can't be confirmed it could have been filmed on The Ridgeway in Enfield across the road from where they suck water from the bus radiator via a tube.

The second series episode, *The Used Combination*, sees Stan, Olive and Mum push the motorbike and sidecar up a very steep road lined by trees and I suspect this was filmed in Harrow on the Hill on Sudbury Hill and the second scene where they push the vehicle up a road lined by houses, which I'd again suspect was filmed in the same area but with far less of an incline in the street.

Into Series Three and this is the first of the rural locations. In *First Aid*, a passenger goes into labour on Stan's bus and Jack rings the bell to stop the bus as it travels along a country lane lined by trees. There are no real clues to this location but I would say it is quite possibly a rural-looking lane in a suburb of London, as it looks quite busy with traffic for a rural location.

Another rural location arises in *Foggy Night*, when Stan's bus drops off the family in a country lane with woodland on either side of the road. Initially, I thought this may have been filmed on Hampstead Heath but that was ruled out on closer inspection, as was Epping Forest. Quite possibly this was filmed in Enfield on the outskirts of London.

The first undiscovered location from Series Four is another rural location in the episode *Nowhere to Go*. Arthur, Olive and Mum travel along a country lane lined by hedges on the repaired motorbike and sidecar when they have an accident. My most-favoured likely location for this scene is Osterley Lane in Norwood Green, London but cannot confirm it one way or the other.

The only other location as yet unfound in Series Four is from *Christmas Duty*, when we see firemen smashing a rear window to extinguish a fire. If this was not filmed in the studios then I'd say a good candidate for this location would be the rear of No. 39 Alric Avenue in Brent, as the policeman is seen entering a back gate at this property earlier in the episode. If this is a direct continuation then my hunch is correct but I will let you judge for yourselves.

The next unknown location crops up in the first episode of Series Six in *No Smoke Without Fire*, and yet again this is a rural location. We see Stan and Jack aboard a bus when a fire breaks out on it as it travels along a tree-lined country lane before turning left into a field, where the bus burns down in spectacular fashion after Blakey is rescued via the rear window upstairs. The countryside north of Enfield and along the northernmost parts of London had been scoured for this location without success but I do now believe it may have been filmed in the Denham area – a village just to the north-west of London.

The episode *Private Hire*, later in Series Six, contains an unknown location. We see Stan and Jack carrying furniture out of a house to load onto their bus with red-bricked houses in the background with distinctive turret-like structures on them. I am confident this was filmed in the Crouch End area as other locations found in this episode were filmed here.

Moving onto Series Seven where these locations will no doubt be found south of the Thames and in the second episode of the series, called *The Perfect Clippie*, Jack is ticked off by Olive for smoking upstairs as the bus passes a large white office block. This office block resembles Shell House on York Road near Waterloo Station and they did film in this area for this episode. Moments later, Jack has just complained to Stan and as he re-enters the bus Olive ticks him off again as we see a large and old church in the background which I believe is somewhere in the Kennington area. In the same episode the bus pulls up at a terminus that looks to be at an old-style shopping precinct, which I'd presume has now been redeveloped and may have been in Lambeth.

The majority of the next batch of unknown locations are likely to have been in the West Sussex countryside east of the town of Haywards Heath which featured in the Series Seven episode *On the Omnibuses*. An exhibition of antique buses is held at the bus depot and I am fairly confident this would have been filmed in the backyard of the Nunhead Lane bus depot in Peckham, which has since been demolished. At the beginning of Stan's dream we see Stan and Jack with their horse-drawn bus passing railway arches and a viaduct and I'd guess this would have been filmed in the Nunhead area. Later, Mum is seen with laundry, waiting by the roadside of a country lane with what looks like a stream behind her as the bus nears. This may have been filmed on Sloop Lane a few miles to the east of Haywards Heath – a location known to be used in this episode. When Mum goes upstairs on the bus with her laundry it looks like this was filmed at a different location but I'd confidently say it would be in the same area. The depot manager is later seen travelling along a country lane in his chauffeur-driven car and in the background it looks like a dairy farm can be seen. This could be Freshfield Mill Farm which is just off Sloop Lane east of Haywards Heath. Still, in *On the Omnibuses*, we see the omnibus driven by Stan heading down a country lane, causing a woman pushing a pram in the middle of the road to hurry along. Again, this is likely to be in the same piece of countryside as the earlier locations in this episode. Likewise, when we see Blakey peddling on his bike, discovering laundry scattered on the road, it is a rural location with a field in the background with a new-looking black fence around it, so maybe a field for horses, again likely to be in the same area. A night shot of the depot manager's car travelling along a lane before crashing into the side of Stan's bus towards the end of the episode looks like a railway line runs parallel to the road here, but again this would have been in the same West Sussex countryside.

The final undiscovered location from the television series comes in the Series Seven episode, *The Allowance*. Olive and Jessie exit a park building that does look like public toilets with an archway, but I have my doubts these were actually toilets, as a seating area can be seen at the rear which is highly unlikely to be found at toilets. Many public parks have been scoured in South London for this distinctive building, without success. I feel that Peckham Common or Morden Hall Park are the likeliest of places to find this building.

The spin-off films' unsolved locations begin with the scene in the 1971 *On the Buses* film when Stan and Arthur enter the backyard of the Butler house to see what can be done about Arthur's motorbike and sidecar. I'd be surprised if this was filmed at the rear of 2 Malden Road and would be confident in saying this was shot at the studios, along with all internal shots of the Butler house. Later in the film, when a bus pulls up at the hospital with the sidecar aboard, with Olive in labour, this was not an actual hospital. This scene was filmed on studio grounds with the exterior of the building containing Stages 1, 2, 3 and 4 doubling as the hospital. These were demolished in the early 1990s to make way for the Tesco Extra store and its car park which stands there to this day. Also in this film, when a bus is diverted onto the motorway, this scene was filmed on the slip road leading onto the A1 northbound. Directly east of the location now is Sullivan Buses depot at South Mimms and can be pinpointed by the flyovers ahead and to the rear of the bus. Photographing of this location was to prove impossible and so this location was omitted from the known locations section.

Onto *Mutiny on the Buses* and Olive is on her way to the depot aboard Arthur's motorbike and sidecar. She rounds a bend with a house on the corner and I am pretty confident this was filmed at the very top of Bullhead Road with the house on the corner being No. 201. Interior locations filmed at Windsor Safari Park have obviously changed so much, as the attraction closed and it was to be replaced by LegoLand. The grand white building seen in the background is St Leonard's Mansion but today it is now hidden from view by trees. You will have noticed I have included a couple of external locations of the former safari park earlier in the book and a couple of behind the scenes shots in a break from filming *Mutiny on the Buses*.

**Reg Varney and Stephen Lewis take a break
from filming at Windsor Safari Park.**

The final spin-off film, *Holiday on the Buses*, contains the greatest number of unknown locations by some distance, but this is to be expected as the majority of the film was filmed on location in North Wales. However, one of the first locations to figure in the film was the Department of Employment building that we see Stan and Jack queueing outside, bumping into Blakey and this location is seen again at the end of the film. This was filmed outside the east of Stages 7 and 8 at Elstree Studios, which is a part of the studios that escaped demolition in the

1990s but it is impossible to gather photographs for this location as Elstree Studios' strict security protocols prevent access.

At the holiday camp we see Stan on the phone to Arthur and this looks to have been filmed in the reception area by a flight of stairs, but this area has undergone redevelopment so pinpointing this location has proved impossible. In a brief scene we see Stan's bus travelling along a country road, perhaps having just crossed a flyover or bridge and I suspect this may have been filmed on St Asaph Road near the town of Rhuddlan before we cut to the family aboard the motorbike and sidecar on their way to the holiday camp.

Reg and Stephen clowning around in the lion's enclosure.

As part of the mystery tour, Stan is seen driving his bus along a narrow lane with a stony wall running along the roadside in what looks to be a hilly location. I believe this was filmed on either Hillside or Allt Y Graig on the hills that overlook Prestatyn.

A location seen on three occasions in the film is an area in the main building at the holiday camp. A wall painted orange with arrows directing holidaymakers to the restaurant and cafeteria, to Snowdonia Bar and to the ballroom is first seen as Stan and Jack contemplate going in to pester Blakey as he gives dance lessons. It is virtually certain this location is unrecognisable today and I'd guess this corridor was somewhere in what is now the reception area. The corridor ran along the back of a flight of stairs which still remain in the reception area but have been moved over the years and is seen again when Olive has to use the toilets in the main building. Later in the film we see an old Sealink ferry in very rough seas which was likely just stock footage held by the studios and all scenes aboard the ferry would have been filmed at the studios.

We see Stan and Jack visit a goods store at the camp for paint and a new toilet and this area was, at the time, being used as the staff canteen. This building can still be found to the far west of the holiday camp with Prestatyn Town's football ground to its west. Internally, this building was also used for filming, with the canteen and kitchen scenes being filmed within. The hatch which Stan gets pulled through remained here until early in 2015 when it was finally removed. In a strange twist of fate, all these years later, the building is now used as a store for camp equipment and is now strictly out of bounds to the public but can be photographed from afar.

It is back to Borehamwood for another location that is known but has changed to such a degree a photograph of the location would not mean a lot. The scene where Blakey sleeps on a deckchair as little Arthur ties a rope to the deckchair with the other end tied to a donkey before firing a cap gun to alarm the poor animal, was filmed on the grounds of Elstree Studios and not at the holiday camp, as was long thought to be the case. The clue is when you see Blakey from a side-on view with Olive and Arthur also sleeping in deckchairs beside him. In the background, the rear of houses can be seen and these have been identified as the rear of Nos. 29, 31 and 33 Whitehouse Avenue in Borehamwood. When Blakey is dragged along by the donkey the scene cuts to the next scene as we see the rear of No. 21 Whitehouse Avenue in the background. Today this area is part of the Tesco Extra car park with the rear of those properties on Whitehouse Avenue concealed by a tall fence and trees.

Towards the end of *Holiday on the Buses* we see the family departing the holiday camp aboard the motorbike and sidecar. The stretch of road this was filmed on was just to the right of the main building up to what were the first aid rooms and I have chosen to omit this entry from the known locations as it is seen throughout the book and in other scenes.

Finally, in the last scene, as the closing credits are set to roll, we see Stan in his new job in demolition. He is seen knocking down what looks like the old bus depot as he looks very pleased with himself. Some have thought this was actually the exact same building (Stage 5 at Elstree Studios) but this could not be the case as Stage 5 was not demolished until the early 1990s to make way for the Tesco Extra store which stands there today, although it is feasible it could have been a sound stage at Borehamwood's MGM Studios (possibly Stage 5) that once stood on Elstree Way less than a mile to the east of Elstree Studios, which closed in 1970.

The rear of houses on Whitehouse Avenue can be seen in the background and where Blakey is seated is now the car park of Tesco Extra in Borehamwood.

Stan destroying what was Stage 5 at the old British-MGM Studios in Borehamwood which closed in 1970.

Travel and Trip Suggestions

If you plan to visit any of the locations that feature in this book then here I will offer a few tips and suggestions to help you on your travels.

First of all, at the time of going to print all of my public transport tips on how to reach each filming location were correct. However, it is inevitable that some details may alter over time as railway franchises change, so the train operating companies may differ from those I have listed, but your end destination will remain the same. It is also possible that engineering work on the rail or underground network on the date you choose to travel may mean you have to find alternative routes to the locations. The same applies to the bus services and suggested routes. I would recommend that you purchase an Oyster Card if you plan on using public transport to reach the filming locations, as it will allow you to reach the majority of the filming locations via bus, rail or underground services. By all means, if you prefer an alternative route to these locations, take them, as those offered in this book are merely the quickest perceived route to the filming location. If you intend on travelling to the locations by car then postcodes have been offered to help you find the locations if you intend on using Sat Nav. However, in some instances postcodes may be not totally accurate as some of the locations are remote country lanes without properties nearby to give an accurate postcode, but rest assured those given are in the nearest possible vicinity.

Some of the locations that you visit may not be easily accessible and residents may be alarmed to see their property being openly photographed so please remember to try to respect people's privacy and show courtesy at all times if challenged as to your intentions. Also, please be careful when crossing roads at all times. If you do decide to visit Elstree Studios please take your photographs from outside the studio grounds from Shenley Road. I say this, as if you wander onto studio-owned land with a camera, looking to take photographs, the security staff present will promptly eject you from the site.

If you visit the location of the former London Transport's skidpan facility in Chiswick, this area has changed beyond recognition and to get a photograph of an angle that matches that seen in the film you will be flirting with office blocks belonging to high profile companies, so it may be wise to get clearance or permission to be in the area with your camera. If you are merely visiting the location and not photographing then you should have no problem.

Obviously, if you wish to visit what was once Windsor Safari Park (now Legoland), then the filming locations listed in the book are able to be visited without paying an entrance fee to the resort, but if you intend on retracing the tour bus route inside the park (difficult to do in any case as so much has changed) you will have to pay an admission fee.

The Pontins Prestatyn Sands holiday camp in North Wales is rich in filming locations and well worth a visit. However, if you have not booked to stay at the holiday camp when you visit you will need to purchase a day pass to gain access to the camp and be warned about photography here. This camp has children's events and you do need to be careful what you are seen to be photographing in this day and age. The photographing of the swimming pool will not be allowed when it is in public use, so if you wish to take photographs of this area seek permission from security staff or management who will advise you of an appropriate time. Also, there are a few filming locations in the camp listed in this book which are out of bounds to the public. The first aid rooms, former staff canteen and its kitchen area are all locations which you will only be able to get access to if you contact management or security, preferably in advance of your visit to the camp.

With just over two hundred filming locations listed to visit, I felt that a welcome addition to the book would be trip suggestions to advise you when visiting a certain area to take in as large a number of locations in one visit as possible. I have included these trip suggestions below, listing each location you can visit using the railway stations you disembark from as a focal point (accept for the village of Shenley), with these listed in alphabetical order.

A Bumper Borehamwood Weekend

The Hertfordshire town of Borehamwood is where a large percentage of filming locations from the spin-off films are to be found. These are dotted across the town and if you wish to visit them all in one trip I'd recommend a weekend stay in the town. Below are the locations that you can visit, beginning with those ranging closest to Elstree and Borehamwood's railway station down to those furthest away.

Location 158: The Gasworks.
Station Road, Borehamwood, Hertfordshire, WD6 1GR.

Location 92: Opening Credits – On the Buses.
Shenley Road, Borehamwood, Hertfordshire, WD6 1AD.

Location 137: Theme Score Strikes Up.
Shenley Road, Borehamwood, Hertfordshire, WD6 1AH.

Location 160: Dustbins Knocked Over.
Clarendon Road, Borehamwood, Hertfordshire, WD6 1BE.

Location 98: Opening Credits – The Butler House.
Malden Road, Borehamwood, Hertfordshire, WD6 1BW.

Location 96: Opening Credits – Introducing Jack.
Cardinal Avenue, Borehamwood, Hertfordshire, WD6 1ER.

Location 138: Payne the Jeweller.
Shenley Road, Borehamwood, Hertfordshire, WD6 1AH.

Location 97: Opening Credits – Roy Skeggs.
Shenley Road, Borehamwood, Hertfordshire, WD6 1EF.

Location 99: Opening Credits – Approaching Turnaround Point.
Whitehouse Avenue, Borehamwood, Hertfordshire, WD6 1HA.

Location 100: Turnaround Betty's House.
Whitehouse Avenue, Borehamwood, Hertfordshire, WD6 1HD.

Location 132: St Luke's Maternity Hospital.
Shenley Road, Borehamwood, Hertfordshire, WD6 1EQ.

Location 101: The Family Planning Clinic.
Shenley Road, Borehamwood, Hertfordshire, WD6 1JG.

Location 91: Stan and Jack Ogle a Clippie.
Tesco Superstore, Shenley Road, Borehamwood, Hertfordshire, WD6 1JG.

Location 90: Elstree Studios.
Shenley Road, Borehamwood, Hertfordshire, WD6 1JG.

Location 135: Buses Parked Back-to-Back.
Brook Road, Borehamwood, Hertfordshire, WD6 5HG.

Location 134: The Closing Credits.
Brook Road, Borehamwood, Hertfordshire, WD6 5EQ.

Location 136: A Third Bus Arrives on the Scene.
Brodewater Road, Borehamwood, Hertfordshire, WD6 5AJ.

Location 170: Broken Down Motorbike and Sidecar.
Barnet Lane, Borehamwood, Hertfordshire, WD6 3JF.

Location 148: Towing Continues.
Bullhead Road, Borehamwood, Hertfordshire, WD6 1HW.

Location 155: Arthur Rescued.
Bullhead Road, Borehamwood, Hertfordshire, WD6 1HS.

Location 147: Motorbike and Sidecar Towed Uphill.
Bullhead Road, Borehamwood, Hertfordshire, WD6 1HT.

Location 153: The Workman's Tent.
Bullhead Road, Borehamwood, Hertfordshire, WD6 1HS.

Location 154: Olive Stuck in a Manhole.
Bullhead Road, Borehamwood, Hertfordshire, WD6 1HS.

Location 151: Brace for Impact.
Bullhead Road, Borehamwood, Hertfordshire, WD6 1HP.

Location 139: Motorbike and Sidecar Travelling Downhill.
Bullhead Road, Borehamwood, Hertfordshire, WD6 1HP.

Location 149: Towed to the Top of the Hill.
Bullhead Road, Borehamwood, Hertfordshire, WD6 1HT.

Location 150: Approaching a Traffic Island.
Bullhead Road, Borehamwood, Hertfordshire, WD6 1HR.

Location 152: Bus Pulls into a Side Street.
Kenilworth Drive, Borehamwood, Hertfordshire, WD6 1QD.

Location 161: Crossing the Traffic Island.
Bullhead Road, Borehamwood, Hertfordshire, WD6 1RQ.

Location 133: Sally's House.
Bullhead Road, Borehamwood, Hertfordshire, WD6 1RJ.

Location 111: A Bus with Spiders Aboard.
Leeming Road, Borehamwood, Hertfordshire, WD6 4EB.

Location 121: A Trip to Hospital for a Check-up.
Leeming Road, Borehamwood, Hertfordshire, WD6 4DY.

Location 159: The Estate Agent.
Aycliffe Road, Borehamwood, Hertfordshire, WD6 4EG.

Location 156: Policemen in Patrol Car Contacted by Mistake.
Torworth Road, Borehamwood, Hertfordshire, WD6 4EY.

Location 140: A Close-Up of the Motorbike and Sidecar.
Gateshead Road, Borehamwood, Hertfordshire, WD6 5DZ.

Location 141: Introducing Arthur.
Gateshead Road, Borehamwood, Hertfordshire, WD6 5LW.

Location 113: Swerving Bus.
Gateshead Road, Borehamwood, Hertfordshire, WD6 5DZ.

Location 115: Bus Continues to Swerve.
Gateshead Road, Borehamwood, Hertfordshire, WD6 5LL.

Location 114: Policeman Directs Traffic.
Gateshead Road, Borehamwood, Hertfordshire, WD6 5LZ.

Location 112: Itching Legs.
Gateshead Road, Borehamwood, Hertfordshire, WD6 5LJ.

Location 116: Bus Crashes into Truck.
Stanborough Avenue, Borehamwood, Hertfordshire, WD6 5LP.

Location 102: Approaching the Launderette.
Manor Way, Borehamwood, Hertfordshire, WD6 1QR.

Location 103: Stopping at the Launderette.
Manor Way, Borehamwood, Hertfordshire, WD6 1QX.

Location 104: The Knicker-Snatcher Scene.
Manor Way, Borehamwood, Hertfordshire, WD6 1QX.

Location 157: Policeman on his Beat Contacted by Mistake.
Manor Way, Borehamwood, Hertfordshire, WD6 1QX.

Location 142: Jack Collecting Fares.
Manor Way, Borehamwood, Hertfordshire, WD6 2AA.

Location 94: Opening Credits – Introducing Mum and Arthur.
Rossington Avenue, Borehamwood, Hertfordshire, WD6 4LA.

Location 93: Opening Credits – Not Stopping for Passengers.
Rossington Avenue, Borehamwood, Hertfordshire, WD6 4LA.

Location 110: The Third Diversion Sign.
Cromwell Road, Borehamwood, Hertfordshire, WD6 4LW.

Location 109: The Second Diversion Sign.
Cromwell Road, Borehamwood, Hertfordshire, WD6 4LN.

Location 108: Following the First Diversion Sign.
Cromwell Road, Borehamwood, Hertfordshire, WD6 4LJ.

Location 107: The First Diversion Sign.
Gateshead Road, Borehamwood, Hertfordshire, WD6 5LJ.

Location 106: False Diversions Await.
Wetherby Road, Borehamwood, Hertfordshire, WD6 4LH.

Location 95: Opening Credits – Introducing Blakey.
Thirsk Road, Borehamwood, Hertfordshire, WD6 5AX.

Location 124: The Journey to Hospital Resumes.
Cowley Hill, Borehamwood, Hertfordshire, WD6 5ND.

The Prestatyn and North Wales Tour

In order to take in the many filming locations in North Wales I would recommend a weekend break at Pontins Prestatyn Sands camp. It will enable you to visit the many locations dotted around the holiday camp and act as a good base to visit locations that are dotted around the surrounding North Wales countryside. If you do opt for a stay in a local hotel then be prepared, as you will need to buy a day pass to gain entrance into the holiday camp. The list of locations is once more listed in closest proximity to Prestatyn's railway station first and spanning outwards.

Location 175: The Family Arrive.
Barkby Avenue, Prestatyn, Denbighshire, LL19 7LA.

Location 165: Main Gates at Pontins Prestatyn Sands Camp.
Barkby Avenue, Prestatyn, Denbighshire, LL19 7LA.

Location 166: Stan Meets Blakey.
Barkby Avenue, Prestatyn, Denbighshire, LL19 7LA.

Location 168: Meet the Camp Nurse.
Barkby Avenue, Prestatyn, Denbighshire, LL19 7LA.

Location 193: The Waiting Room.
Barkby Avenue, Prestatyn, Denbighshire, LL19 7LA.

Location 194: The Treatment Room.
Barkby Avenue, Prestatyn, Denbighshire, LL19 7LA.

Location 199: Mr Coombs Berates Inspector Blake.
Barkby Avenue, Prestatyn, Denbighshire, LL19 7LA.

Location 178: The Swimming Pool.
Barkby Avenue, Prestatyn, Denbighshire, LL19 7LA.

Location 200: Blakey Confronts Stan.
Barkby Avenue, Prestatyn, Denbighshire, LL19 7LA.

Location 169: Mavis and her Mum aboard a Tricycle.
Barkby Avenue, Prestatyn, Denbighshire, LL19 7LA.

Location 201: The Boating Lake.
Barkby Avenue, Prestatyn, Denbighshire, LL19 7LA.

Location 202: Exiting the Boating Lake.
Barkby Avenue, Prestatyn, Denbighshire, LL19 7LA.

Location 167: Inspecting the Staff.
Barkby Avenue, Prestatyn, Denbighshire, LL19 7LA.

Location 164: The Main Building at Pontins Prestatyn Sands Camp.
Barkby Avenue, Prestatyn, Denbighshire, LL19 7LA.

Location 192: Exiting the Amusement Arcade.
Barkby Avenue, Prestatyn, Denbighshire, LL19 7LA.

Location 203: The Chase Continues.
Barkby Avenue, Prestatyn, Denbighshire, LL19 7LA.

Location 204: Sacked.
Barkby Avenue, Prestatyn, Denbighshire, LL19 7LA.

Location 177: The Bar Area.
Barkby Avenue, Prestatyn, Denbighshire, LL19 7LA.

Location 191: Dance Rehearsals.
Barkby Avenue, Prestatyn, Denbighshire, LL19 7LA.

Location 176: The Butler Chalet.
Barkby Avenue, Prestatyn, Denbighshire, LL19 7LA.

Location 196: Stan, Jack and a Toilet.
Barkby Avenue, Prestatyn, Denbighshire, LL19 7LA.

Location 197: Wally Leads Lily to the Toilet in the Bushes.
Barkby Avenue, Prestatyn, Denbighshire, LL19 7LA.

Location 190: Stan Visits Mavis in her Chalet.
Barkby Avenue, Prestatyn, Denbighshire, LL19 7LA.

Location 195: The Exploding Drains.
Barkby Avenue, Prestatyn, Denbighshire, LL19 7LA.

Location 205: The Beached Bus.
Barkby Beach, Prestatyn, Denbighshire, LL19 7LB.

Location 206: Checking on the Beached Bus.
Barkby Beach, Prestatyn, Denbighshire, LL19 7LB.

Location 198: The Manager's House.
Hillside, Prestatyn, Denbighshire, LL19 9PW.

Location 187: Low-Level Bridge.
Allt Y Graig, Dyserth, Denbighshire, LL18 6DE.

Location 188: Overhanging Trees Play Havoc.
Allt Y Graig, Dyserth, Denbighshire, LL18 6DE.

Location 189: Removing the Branches.
Allt Y Graig, Dyserth, Denbighshire, LL18 6DE.

Location 184: Olive Exits a Shop in a Rush.
The Waterfall Shop, Waterfall Road, Dyserth, Denbighshire, LL18 6ET.

Location 183: Blakey Buys Joan an Ice Cream.
Dyserth Falls, Waterfall Road, Dyserth, Denbighshire, LL18 6ET.

Location 182: The Waterfall Stop.
Dyserth Falls, Waterfall Road, Dyserth, Denbighshire, LL18 6ET.

Location 179: The Mystery Tour Begins.
High Street, Rhyl, Denbighshire, LL18 1ET.

Location 180: Along the Seafront.
West Parade, Rhyl, Denbighshire, LL18 1HG.

Location 181: Crossing a Bridge.
Rhyl Fford Harbour Bridge, Wellington Road, Rhyl, Denbighshire, LL18 5BQ.

Location 172: On the Approach to the Bridge.
High Street, Rhuddlan, Denbighshire, LL18 2UD.

Location 173: Lost Luggage.
The Rhuddlan Bridge, Station Road, Rhuddlan, Denbighshire, LLU 5UA.

Location 174: Retrieving the Cases.
River Clwyd, Rhuddlan Bridge, Station Road, Denbighshire, LLU 5UA.

Location 171: Holiday Village Road Sign.
St Asaph Road, Rhuddlan, Denbighshire, LL18 5UG.

Location 185: Taking a U-turn on the Motorway.
St Asaph Road, Rhuddlan, Denbighshire, LL18 5UG.

Location 186: Heading down a Country Lane.
Unnamed Lane off St Asaph Road, Rhuddlan, Denbighshire, LL18 5UG.

The Tour of Wembley – The First Home of *On the Buses*

Wembley is a special suburb of London in that it is where *On the Buses* was filmed at the first home of LWT. A full day will be needed to visit all of the known filming locations in the area and these are listed in order of closest proximity to Wembley Park Underground Station.

Location 31: Stan Pays a Gas Bill.
Olympic Way, Wembley, London, HA9 0UU.

Location 1: The Former LWT Studios.
128 Wembley Park Drive, Wembley, London, HA9 8HP.

Location 2: The Opening Credits in Series One Start.
Wembley Park Drive, Wembley, London, HA9 8HD.

Location 48: The Dressmaker's Dummy at a Bus Stop.
Vivian Avenue, Wembley, London, HA9 6RH.

Location 49: Blakey Finds the Dressmaker's Dummy.
Vivian Avenue, Wembley, London, HA9 6RQ.

Location 16: Stan Shopping on Duty.
Harrow Road, Wembley, London, HA9 6PG.

Location 19: Arthur Receives Tools.
East Lane, Wembley, London, HA0 3NJ.

Location 20: Arthur's Motorbike Breaks Down.
East Lane, Wembley, London, HA0 3LF.

Location 21: Bus Towing the Motorbike.
Oldborough Road, Wembley, London, HA0 3PR.

Location 22: The Handlebars Come Off.
Holt Road, Wembley, London, HA0 3PY.

Location 34: Sawdust on Fire.
Holt Road, Wembley, London, HA0 3PS.

Location 33: Arthur's Smoking Motorcycle.
Dean Court, Wembley, London, HA0 3PX.

Location 35: The Missing Sidecar.
Campden Crescent, Wembley, London, HA0 3JQ.

Location 36: The Sidecar is Found.
The Fairway, Wembley, London, HA0 3LJ.

Location 23: Jack Notices the Bike Has Gone.
The Fairway, Wembley, London, HA0 3LP.

A Day Trip to Wood Green and Home to the Original Bus Depot

The North London suburb of Wood Green was frequently visited by the filming crews of *On the Buses* and crucially it was the home of the Eastern National bus depot, which served as the depot of the fictional Luxton and District Company. A day trip to Wood Green should suffice, enabling you to visit each filming location and these are listed on order of their closeness to Wood Green Underground Station.

Location 4: The Luxton and District Bus Depot.
Omnibus House, Lordship Lane, Wood Green, London, N22 5JY.

Location 39: Picking up Stan.
Redvers Road, Wood Green, London, N22 6EQ.

Location 5: The Race to the Rear of the Depot.
Lordship Lane, Wood Green, London, N22 5JN.

Location 42: The Second-Hand Bed Scene.
Albert Vittoria House, Pellatt Grove, Wood Green, London, N22 5PG.

Location 11: Stan Ticks off Clippie.
Perth Road, Wood Green, London, N22 5PX.

Location 12: Stan Suffers Bus Stop Frustration.
Perth Road, Wood Green, London, N22 5PY.

Location 44: The Kids Outing Begins.
Perth Road, Wood Green, London, N22 5PY.

Location 45: The Exhaust Pipe Falls Off.
Berwick Road, Wood Green, London, N22 5QB.

Location 46: Bus Stops and Kids Misbehave.
Inverness Terrace, Wood Green, London, N22 5BT.

Location 8: Olive Feels Unwell.
Palace Gates Road, Wood Green, London, N22 7BW.

Location 9: Olive's Illness Continues.
Palace Gates Road, Wood Green, London, N22 7BW.

Location 3: End of the Opening Credits in Series One.
Alexandra Park Road, Wood Green, London, N10 2DG.

Location 13: Stan Regulates Jack.
Alexandra Park Road, Wood Green, London, N10 2AD.

Nunhead's Bus Depot and the Butler House Tour

The seventh series of *On the Buses* featured a different bus depot located in Nunhead Lane and neighbouring it was a plethora of locations in a small vicinity. This locations trip can certainly be covered in a day and below are the locations listed in order of closeness to Nunhead's railway station.

Location 61: Blakey Escorts Olive Home.
Carden Road, Peckham, London, SE15 3UB.

Location 88: The Rag and Bone Man Arrives.
Carden Road, Peckham, London, SE15 3UD.

Location 62: Sandra's House.
Carden Road, Peckham, London, SE15 3UD.

Location 77: Stan Leaves Luxton.
Nunhead Lane, Peckham, London, SE15 3TU.

Location 78: Turning the Water Mains Off.
Carden Road, Peckham, London, SE15 3UD.

Location 89: Arguing over Manure.
Carden Road, Peckham, London, SE15 3UD.

Location 84: Blakey Takes to his Bike.
East Dulwich Road, Peckham, London, SE15 3UA.

Location 83: Sandra Visiting Public Toilets.
Peckham Rye Park, East Dulwich Road, Peckham, London, SE15 3UA.

Location 79: A Walk to Public Toilets.
Peckham Rye Park, Peckham, London, SE15 3UA.

Location 81: Jessie's Complaint.
Peckham Rye Park, Peckham, London, SE15 3UA.

Location 80: Olive and Jessie Exit Public Toilets.
Peckham Rye Park, Peckham, London, SE15 3UA.

The Unique Potters Bar Tour

This trip is unique amongst those suggested as it is the only tour that covers both filming locations from the television series and the spin-off films. On arriving at Potters Bar you may find there is quite a lot of travelling still to be done, so I'd recommend a full day for this tour and again locations are listed in order of closeness to Potters Bar railway station.

Location 117: Toilet Stop at a Garage.
St Albans Road, South Mimms, Hertfordshire, EN6 3PN.

Location 126: The Hump-Backed Bridge.
Wash Lane, Potters Bar, Hertfordshire, EN6 3QQ.

Location 125: Along a Country Lane.
Wash Lane, Potters Bar, Hertfordshire, EN6 3QQ.

Location 14: A Drink at a Country Cottage.
The Ridgeway, Enfield, London, EN2 8AP.

Location 15: Another Drink from the Radiator.
The Ridgeway, Enfield, London, EN2 8AN.

Location 146: The Farmyard Crash.
Chalk Hill Farm, Ridge, Hertfordshire, EN6 3LP.

Location 130: Another Diversion.
Rowley Lane, Barnet, Hertfordshire, EN5 3HW.

Location 131: Diverting onto a Motorway.
Rowley Lane, Barnet, Hertfordshire, EN5 3HW.

The Shenley Village Tour

The peaceful and picturesque Hertfordshire village of Shenley was a popular place for the filming crews of *On the Buses* to venture to for scenes featuring in the spin-off films. Your journey by public transport to Shenley will be by bus from neighbouring Borehamwood but a day should be more than sufficient time to visit all locations. In this instance, the locations are listed in order of closeness to the main street in Shenley – London Road.

Location 119: Toilet in a Public House.
London Road, Shenley, Hertfordshire, WD7 9ER.

Location 122: The Sidecar Problem.
London Road, Shenley, Hertfordshire, WD7 9DX.

Location 123: Hasty Repairs.
Newcome Road, Shenley, Hertfordshire, WD7 9EG.

Location 144: Arthur's Driving Lessons.
Rectory Lane, Shenley, Hertfordshire, WD7 9BX.

Location 127: The Sidecar Splits.
Rectory Lane, Shenley, Hertfordshire, WD7 9BX.

Location 145: Stan Hanging out of the Driver's Cab.
Mimms Lane, Shenley, Hertfordshire, WD7 9AP.

Location 128: The Sidecar Comes to a Stop.
Mimms Lane, Shenley, Hertfordshire, WD7 9AP.

Location 129: Stan Stops a Bus.
Mimms Lane, Shenley, Hertfordshire, WD7 9AP.

Location 120: Country Lane Toilet Stop.
London Road, Shenley, Hertfordshire, WD6 5PH.

Appendix

Well, now that you have read the book, I hope you will take the chance to visit these iconic filming locations. To make your trips as easy as possible and turn back the clock to when some of these locations looked so much more different, I have added in some useful maps and pictures below which I hope will enhance your enjoyment of the book and your trips to the locations.

If you are travelling around London, visiting filming locations, or are out and about and feel the urge to visit some locations then the London Underground map will be of great use. This is available at major underground stations or by consulting www.tfl.gov.uk.

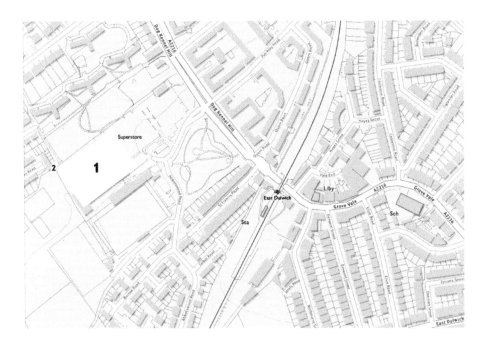

The football pitch used in *The Football Match* episode in Series Seven has long gone but this will give you an idea of where it once stood. The key is: 1. Indicates where the football pitch stood where the Luxton Lions played the Basildon Bashers. 2. The precise location of the changing rooms. A Sainbury's superstore and car park now occupies the site.

The EMI-MGM Elstree Studios were once a vast site, spreading across land where a Tesco Extra and its car park now stands. This photo shows how the studios once looked, with the area outlined in white being the part of the studio site that was demolished in the early 1990s. A useful key to relevant *On the Buses* information is as follows:

1. Stage 5 (served as the bus depot in the spin-off films)

2. The Family Planning Clinic

3. The Hospital Entrance

4. St. Luke's Maternity Hospital Exit

5. Blakey dragged along in his deckchair scene.

6. The Department of Employment offices

In the first spin-off film, the old London Transport skidpan facility at Chiswick features in the film. Sadly, this was demolished many years ago but this old photograph gives you an idea of what the site looked like from above. The road at the bottom of the photo is Chiswick High Road.

If you wish to retrace the tour bus route around Windsor Safari Park (now Legoland) it has changed beyond recognition, but this old map of the park that features in *Mutiny on the Buses* may help.

A map of Prestatyn to enable you to find your way from the train station to the Prestatyn Sands holiday camp.

The Prestatyn Sands holiday camp, run by Pontins, features in *Holiday on the Buses*. If you decide to visit the camp this map will be of use to you. The points of interest are:

1. Camp Gates

2. Security Office

3. First Aid Room

4. Swimming Pool

5. Main Building

6. Camp Stores

7. Boating Pond

8. Blakey gets sacked

9. The Exploding Drain

10. The Butler Chalet

PRINTED AND BOUND BY:
Copytech (UK) Limited trading as Printondemand-worldwide,
9 Culley Court, Bakewell Road, Orton Southgate.
Peterborough, PE2 6XD, United Kingdom.